WHY DO INDIANS ... ?

WHY DO INDIANS ... ?

A Contemporary Perspective
on Inscrutable Indian Ways

Vivek Vaidya

PARTRIDGE

You can reach Vivek Vaidya at www.vivekvaidya.com mr.vivekvaidya@gmail.com
Facebook: whydoindians

Print information available on the last page.

To order additional copies of this book, contact
Toll Free 800 101 2657 (Singapore)
Toll Free 1 800 81 7340 (Malaysia)
orders.singapore@partridgepublishing.com

www.partridgepublishing.com/singapore

CONTENTS

DEDICATED

to

All My International Friends

Who Asked Me Difficult Questions

&

Those Innumerable Blog Readers

Who Appreciated My Perspectives

ACKNOWLEDGMENTS

I must acknowledge that I am most nervous writing this section of the book. There are number of people involved in making this venture a reality and I am nervous that I may miss out someone. Still, let me try.

Firstly, I must acknowledge the innumerable blog readers, who read my blog regularly and actively communicate their opinions. Without this community, I would have got the confidence to write anything.

I wrote this book mostly while travelling in public transport, while waiting at the airport or while flying. I then shared it with my friends for friendly critique. Thanks Amar, Sameer, and Sunil for initial feedback and encouragement. Thanks Aparna for diving deep into my story characters and helping me fine-tune them. Thanks Dushyant and Deven for giving valuable inputs. Thanks Vrushali and Madhavi for being such strong promoter of my blogs and critiquing my efforts. Thanks Shilpa, Pratap and Prerna for constantly telling me that I can do it. Special thanks to Sharva for giving me the younger generation's perspective.

Thanks Aprajita and Puneet for spending your valuable time to assure me that my literary effort was worthwhile. I profusely thank

Madhumathi and Namita for their thorough editing and improvement suggestions. The book would not have been as readable without stupendous editing efforts from Tara Dhar Hasnain. Heartfelt thanks to my twelve year old nephew, Manas, too for his valuable proofreading.

Words are not enough to thank my teacher and inspiration Avinash Dharmadhikari (Avida) for writing the foreword. Thanks to Google and Apple for all the technological empowerment, which made this book possible. Thanks to my employer Frost & Sullivan for giving me the opportunity to travel and experience many cultures.

Finally, thanks to my wife Nalini, for pushing me to explore my full potential, for telling me when it wasn't good enough, for helping me not to fall prey to my own impatience and of course for the most apt front & back cover design. Without you, this book would have never been a reality.

PREFACE

It is almost a decade since I started living outside India. In the last decade, I travelled extensively across the world, interacted with colleagues, clients and business associates from various continents, countries & cultures.

As interactions became deeper and thicker, acquaintances became friendships and they started asking me all the questions they had in their minds about us 'Indians'; questions about things that we do differently than rest of the world that shock and puzzle them. They are shocked that arranged marriage is still practiced in modern India and beef is banned in some parts of India. They are puzzled about cricket and movies being followed like religions.

Sometimes these questions arose out of outdated stereotypes, sometimes from direct experience and sometimes out of genuine curiosity. Initially, I laughed at them, then I ducked them but then I sensed that not answering them has its flipside that the outdated stereotypes continue. So I asked fellow Indians and they had similar experiences. Everyone had questions but nobody had any answers.

In a classical Hindu philosophical way, when I could not find the answers in the outer world, I turned inwards for the answers. I got arranged married; I become hysterical during cricket season; I turned non-vegetarian but still can't bring myself to eat beef. So if my international colleagues have questions about these, then I should have answers. With this thought I wrote a blog-series about these questions and possible answers. The blog series turned out to be immensely successful around the world. So I decided to convert the series into a book. Blogs have limitations on words, hence imagination. In this book, I could build entertaining semi- fictional stories around these core questions that have characters and situations you can easily relate to. The characters and situations may be imaginary but the message is real.

I don't claim to have exact answers to all these questions. What I have is my own perspective, reasoning and logic. Most non-Indian readers would also get a sneak preview about what goes on in a rational, global Indian's mind when he is confronted with such questions.

Enjoy my maiden attempt at book-writing and let me know if you like it on www.vivekvaidya.com or www.facebook.com/mr.vivekvaidya

FOREWORD

I have the pleasure of knowing Vivek since he was a school kid. I remember him as an extraordinary intelligent and innocent kid – what a captivating combination! Then over these years he developed into an excellent international professional. It's a great pleasure to see that he has retained, maintained – in fact carefully nurtured his intelligence and innocence. I saw him as the Global Indian. That's the beauty and strength of being Indian. Being Indian doesn't create an either or situation – you can either be Indian or Global – flexible and all-encompassing nature of being Indian, freely lets you be global – at one and the same time. The very essence of being Indian is in this ancient concept of the whole world as one nation – in fact, the whole world as one family.

Vivek is acutely perceptive in 5 dimensions of being Indian – that are present here. Cow-worship, religious devotion to cricket, inexplicable mystique of arranged marriage, infatuation with movies (Bollywood) and quintessential Indian quality of finding creative solutions – the 'Jugaad' – all come out here in their international set up. He uses language keenly, defines characters precisely and builds events graphically. There is every reason to look forward to ever creative expression from Vivek. I enjoyed reading this. Hope you, too, will. Best wishes for one (Vivek) and all (of you).

- Avinash Dharmadhikari
Founder Director Of Chanakya Mandal Parivar
Former Indian Administrative Services officer, Journalist & Activist

REVIEWS

Aditya Kuvalekar - New York, USA - "A lovely read. Vivek throws light on some of the uniquely desi traits that, by now, are our second nature. Be it with obsession with Cricket or the movies, there's something very Indian about us that Vivek investigates and does so through the eyes of a management consultant. What comes out then is a totally rational, reasonable and perhaps a very calculated way of thinking about why we, as Indians, do a few things the way we do. And while we are celebrating quintessentially Indian traits, *Jugaad* can never be left out and it isn't. And here too, like every other story, Vivek brings out a totally new perspective telling us why we need to think beyond *Jugaad* . All in all, a seemingly casual but a thought-provoking book."

Srinivas Raghavan - Mumbai, India - "I am not a bookaholic. However, this is the first book in ten years that arrested my attention completely. The only way to close it was to read it till the end. A high class attempt at exploratory analysis of real time feelings & emotions and intellectual banter. Way to go Vivek"

Aparna Datar - Nagoya, Japan - "Vivek's writing is often representative of all the questions the Japanese media has about Indians. They have a patient, amused and sometimes an incredulous tenor at all the obvious misgivings and curiosities about the Indian ways. The book is a representative of the Indian business traveller's own curiosity at, no matter how global or multicultural Indian sensibilities or consumption evolves into, we like the differentiator that we have to offer to the world beyond being the world's largest economy, our way of life. We are like this ...Only!"

Madhumathi Lakshmi - Bangalore, India - "The 'why's' are an integral part of living and it's believed (by Indians of course, who else:)) that the answers come to us when we are ready. Looks like we are - a thoroughly enjoyable read and enough AHA moments for all - the Indians and the not so. While providing a perspective, I believe the ideas get us thinking about 'ourselves' and our 'way of life' and at least for me leaves a great after taste with a feeling of 'Ok, that makes sense'. Happy reading!"

Vrushali Kulkarni - Hong Kong - "Filled with humour, some serious soul searching, introspection, revisiting the mythological stories and suggestions for the young desi entrants in the global market, the book has everything!"

Shruti Utgikar - Pune, India - "Why do Indians - is an exciting read that actually makes reader live experiences narrated therein. Author has tried to explore rationale behind unique ways Indians live their life. Book is very gripping and gives readers a perspective about diverse global cultures. Is serves as a an excellent referral to Indians for their maiden travel abroad to avoid any potential pitfalls."

Sharva Vaidya - Singapore - "This book was really insightful and gave clear answers for the questions that Indians get asked by foreigners in everyday life. In addition, the stories are written in such a way that every person, Indian or foreigner, young or old, can understand them. It is a great collection of stories that perfectly bridges the gap between cultures."

Namrata Joshi - Bangalore, India - "Why do Indians..." is a very interesting read and attempts to answers some existential questions which we often wondered about or just took them as our way of life... The questions are endearing and stories to the answers are quite entertaining and will keep you hooked till you reach the end of a chapter. At the end you might just have your "aha" moments, while thinking 'yeah, perhaps that's why we do it'. I thoroughly enjoyed reading the story weaved in behind every question and couldn't stop till I got the reasoning behind it."

Mrinal Patwardhan - Singapore - "Vivek is a good friend, who always thinks before he speaks. It is evident in his writing too. Detailed, informative, in a simple language without any jargons yet witty and brings smile to your face! Delight to read always!! Good luck for the book and hope we will get to read many more..."

Ravindra Utgikar - Pune, India - "Why do Indians is a remarkable portray of experiences. A compilation of stories bringing to fore a distinct demeanor Indians exhibit that their foreign counterparts find intriguing. With optimal blend of emotions and humor, Vivek strikes personal bond with reader and makes them relive these moments. His ability to capture subtle nuances of Indian customs and its analysis, is what makes this book a gripping read."

1

WHY DO INDIANS NOT EAT BEEF?

October is a great time of year to be in Seoul. I was there on the eve of a prominent conference in which I was the keynote speaker. As usual I had taken the Airport limousine bus, which dropped me close to my hotel, and I had to walk a couple of blocks to reach my hotel. I always look forward to such intimate interactions with a city. A five-minute walk can tell you a lot more about a city than a hundred-page book.

Open blue skies, a chill in the air and bright sunshine welcome you with open arms. Wide, sharp sloping roads are playgrounds for large, swanky cars that zoom past, drawing the admiration and envy of all. They sound like endless ocean waves breaking at the shore. Smart-looking, fashionable and mostly bespectacled young men and women walk briskly, staring into their phones to look occupied.

This background rhythm was often interrupted by loud laughter coming from a group of smokers supposedly out for fresh air but who were polluting the same. A sudden gush of wind and a group of noisy school children emerging out of an underground subway station broke my chain of thought. The spirit of the city was endearing but I had to reach the hotel in time for an official dinner with the other speakers.

Official dinners in this part of the world are true to their name. The dress code is a business suit. The only possible concession is that it is ok not to wear a tie. A stack of business cards and presence of mind are more of the must-have accessories. You are supposed to be present exactly on time and give a formal introduction of yourself and your company. So there I was, dressed in my deep navy blue business suit with a purple tie, adjusting my rimless spectacles while holding my business cards, getting introduced to other speakers as we waited for our transport to arrive.

Mr. Miller was a tall Caucasian man nearing his 50th birthday. A few remaining black hairs peppered his mostly white hair. From the stubble on his chin it was apparent that he was jet- lagged and had spent most of his spare time in bed. Dressed in a rich black jacket with beige colored trousers, he had a loud voice, confident tone and an unmistakable German accent. With over a decade of experience in investment banking and occupying a leadership position in a prominent company, I had no doubt that he was an important man.

Kato-san was a lean and short person well past his 50. A broad forehead, pronounced nose and a wide chin gave him a typical Japanese appearance. He wore a humble but artificial smile and showed uncharacteristic enthusiasm in greeting the delegates. He held his business card with both hands as he introduced himself with his company name first, followed by his surname, followed by his first name. He came from a reputed company, and hence was one of the most sought after persons in the room. However, it was quite clear from his body language that he did not enjoy being the center of attention.

Mr. Rahmat was a stocky Malaysian man, had a slight beard just below his lower lip and wore gold colored spectacles. The spectacles were probably only for short-sightedness as he was wearing them lower on his nose. He tilted his head down to look at me instead of through the glasses.

Mr. Park, the organizer, and his colleague, Ms. Daisy and also a few other colleagues who were too shy to introduce themselves, joined us. Korean organizations irrespective of their size are quite hierarchical. Juniors shudder to interact with outsiders in the presence of their bosses.

Daisy informed us that the transport had arrived and ushered us towards the concierge. We boarded a 10-seater van to go to a nearby restaurant for dinner. Those who boarded the bus first grabbed vantage seats and though they were asking others to sit next to them, were secretly hoping that nobody would accept the invitation. These are some awkward moments and weak links in planning if you are an organizer, and it showed quite clearly on Mr. Park's face. Finally, somehow, all of us settled down. Daisy got on the seat next to the driver and we started off.

We soon left the wide road and went onto the narrow lanes of Seoul. The city looked very different. It was as if we were watching someone we had always seen well dressed and well manicured in pajamas, without a speck of makeup on her. You knew the face but still the appearance startled you. Daisy navigated us through the maze and soon we arrived at the designated restaurant.

It appeared to be a simple family run restaurant. The signboard and everything else was in Korean, so I didn't understand what the name was, and didn't do anything to find out. The restaurant must have been quite popular as there was a small queue of customers waiting to enter. The owner or perhaps the lady manager was dressed in a light green uniform of the restaurant, and she came outside to greet us. She bowed low in greeting. We were ushered into a special room where we had to remove our shoes outside and sit cross-legged for dinner.

Mr. Miller could not hide his surprise at this custom. He was a bit irritated as he was wearing Oxfords. Perhaps this was his first time in Korea, I thought to myself. Kato-san and I were better prepared with our pump shoes. Mr. Rahmat was busy inspecting various certificates displayed behind the counter to ensure that this was a halal certified restaurant. For Malaysians travelling abroad, ensuring the food served is halal is a big deal. The restaurant manager helped us to keep our shoes in a nice wooden stand at the entrance and ushered us in, while simultaneously helping us with our coats.

We sat cross-legged around a low dining table. The room was tastefully designed with a remarkable wooden appearance. A couple of paintings depicting Korean village landscapes in bright colors hung on opposite walls. A small wooden table for the waiters to keep the plates and cutlery was in one corner. The floor had a mahogany colour finish and felt like it was heated.

Each setting was well laid out with a roll of cold towel, steel chopsticks on the right and a soup spoon on our left. The cup for Chinese tea was kept upside down, several small sized snack dishes kept in their customary places and all of this was placed on a tablemat that had bold Korean characters painted in gold. What was slightly different was that at the center of the table there was a metal grill with copper pipes running vertically with a chimney on top. I guessed that we were in one of the famous Korean 'Galbi' restaurants that are famous for their barbecue across Seoul.

Personally, I find such dinners slightly awkward gatherings. They are supposed to ensure people open up to each other, share commonalities and develop rapport, but what actually happens is that people are trying to gauge each other to develop a pseudo hierarchy, nobody is happy with just the current company and current designation, they want to know which school you went to, when you graduated, where you are located, how frequently you travel, where you travel, what watch you are wearing etc. Answers to all of these questions help them form a mental image of people and allow them to place these people in relation to themselves. That relative position determines who they would hang out with, whom they will ask questions or whom they will answer and at whose joke they will laugh the loudest.

Moreover, these gatherings do not suit me. I have boyish looks, black hair and a slight Indian accent. Most of these characteristics do not go well with a senior consulting position. Most times other delegates mistake me for a last minute replacement of the senior keynote speaker. They keep asking me questions that might help them determine my age, how big my company is etc. I tend to think that their curiosity about me is not genuine. I tend to listen more than talk. I tend to curb my natural aggression in such gatherings and try to be a part of the group, rather than try to dominate it.

As I was lost in my thoughts, I didn't notice how much time had passed but the restaurant manager started serving the food. I like Korean food a lot. It is spicy, hot and appeals to all your senses. Korean food is also about abundance and surprises. When you are expecting starters to arrive, a long unending collection of side dishes arrive. There are several interesting dishes, which are hard to pronounce, but are prepared fresh on a daily basis and over a period of time become the signature side dishes of the restaurant. For this dinner, we also were served water colored rice wine, which does not have a particularly strong taste, but it went well with the overall menu.

A few shots of rice wine with the shout '*Gonbae*', which is a call for bottoms up, loosened everyone up. Genuine smiles appeared, body language was much more relaxed and the decibel levels increased. Informal information sharing and curiosity about each other's cultures and countries replaced the predictable business and economy talk.

Miller didn't know much about India or Indians, while Kato-san had spent about six months in New Delhi. He had developed an acquaintance with a family in Delhi during that time and appeared eager to know more about Indian cultures. So after the usual status-gauging questions, we were talking about India and Indian culture, economy and similar subjects. Mr. Rahmat didn't know much about India or Indians but he did not care to ask me anything. He was clearly unhappy about attention a boyish-looking Indian speaker like me hogging from a senior German and Japanese speaker, so he engaged in discussions with Mr. Park and Ms. Daisy. Side dishes got refilled multiple times, starters came and went and soon it was time for the main course.

Mr. Park appeared to be waiting to make some announcement. He chose the time just before the arrival of the main course to announce that this restaurant was most famous for Bulgogi beef and he had taken a liberty to order unlimited servings of this famous beef to please the guests. Kato-san smiled from ear to ear for the first time that evening and Mr. Miller almost clapped. From a corner of my eye I could see that Mr. Rahmat put back the piece of fried egg he had grabbed in his chopsticks to do justice to the Bulgogi beef, which was on its way. Daisy promptly informed us that the guests in her last conference had requested her to bring them back to this restaurant the next day as proof of the quality of her selection.

Tremendous anticipation had built around the dining table as the efficient restaurant manager walked in with marinated beef and placed it on the barbeque grill. It looked like delicious thin slices of red-pink marble with a natural white design. Everyone got ready for the food and started turning their piece of beef over the grill. They started appreciating the quality as they spoke, except me. Mr. Park, alert as ever, realized this and with a question mark on his face asked me, "What is the matter?"

"I don't eat beef," I answered firmly but in a low tone.

Mr. Park's jaw dropped as he murmured something to Daisy, who promptly left, supposedly to fix something for me.

The others realized something was amiss and asked me what had happened.

"I don't eat beef," I said, this time a bit sheepishly.

I was slightly embarrassed, as I had caused some inconvenience to the organizers who had so far made impeccable arrangements. They had verified whether I was a vegetarian. I did mention that I was a non-vegetarian but I didn't tell them that I didn't eat beef. They were bound to take this slip-up seriously and run around more than required, to fix it. The barbeque was still heating up and it was a good 10-15 minutes before the beef would be ready for the other guests, so all the attention was diverted to me.

"Why?" Mr. Miller asked, "It's perhaps the tastiest meat in the world. This meat in particular looks like the most tender beef I have ever seen."

Mr. Miller looked at Mr. Park in appreciation, who bowed a little to accept the compliments. I did not bother to answer this.

But they were in no mood to give up. Rice wine had loosened up all their inhibitions. Mr. Rahmat finally got the chance that he was waiting for. He could join the conversation with Mr. Miller's alliance.

"Usually there are two reasons. It is either religion that prohibits you from eating a particular meat or personal choice. What is your reason?" he asked and glanced around.

Mr. Miller nodded in appreciation. Kato-san chose to stay neutral by avoiding eye contact and turning his piece of beef on the barbecue grill. The connection between choice of meat and religion was new to Mr. Miller but not to Mr. Rahmat.

In Malaysia and Indonesia, most Muslims don't eat pork and they also look for halal certified restaurants, like Mr. Rahmat who had just recently completed his investigation. So usually people in South East Asia are aware of the connection between religion and meat.

"Religion," I answered, "of course, there are many Indians who relish beef. But I am not one among them. Even, some practicing Buddhists in Thailand do not eat beef."

I was beginning to sound desperate. In my mind I resented that Mr. Park had not invited any Thai speaker, who could have been a great ally. I had to face this alone for now. I was secretly hoping that Kato-san's six months in India would have created some soft corner for Indians and he would join the discussion on my side, but for now, he was busy with his beef.

"Muslims consider the pig to be an unclean animal, hence they abstain from it. What is your reason?" Mr. Rahmat looked at the entire group as he said this. He had killed two birds with one stone. He had informed the group that not eating pork was justified, a logical thing to do for Muslims, whereas there was a big question mark over why someone should avoid beef.

"We consider the cow to be a God," I said. I am not sure if this was my desperation or alcohol, but I was trying to put this discussion beyond the realm of reasoning, to save the day. I could hear some sighs, suppressed laughter and hushed voices. I looked around unsuccessfully for eye contact.

Kato-san was still sitting tight on the fence barbecuing his beef. I considered the option of cracking a silly joke and give a different turn to this discussion to rescue myself. But Mr. Miller was not prepared to let his first encounter with an Indian go in vain. I had heard horror stories from my friends about how they were grilled on this topic, but this was my first experience. I also smiled to myself about how appropriate the word 'grilled' was in this case.

Mr. Miller struggled to turn the choice piece of meat on his barbecue around with his steel chopsticks as he asked, "Being a well-educated, rational individual, do you really think cow is God?"

He knew he was asking me an offensive personal question, so he avoided eye contact as he said this. I hated the patronizing tone. I hated the attempt to draw a relationship between education, rationality and religious beliefs. Anyhow, I ignored all of it to take the debate forward.

"No," I continued to march on. I poured myself some rice wine. Mr. Park watched this in horror, since pouring a drink for yourself is a complete no-no in Korea. But I needed some extra fuel for the journey ahead. Incidentally, my speech next day was on the use of Ethanol as a fuel for cars. "If alcohol can drive a car, why can't it drive me," was a random joke, which distracted me, and with great difficulty I controlled my smile A cyclone was developing, with me firmly entrenched at the epicenter.

"....*aano*... Does your religious book...... the Gita... specifically mention that..... cow is a God?" Kato-san dropped his hat in the ring, joining the Miller-Rahmat alliance. Mr. Park was getting more and more uneasy, so he distracted himself by discussing something with Daisy in Korean. I looked at Kato-san with a facial expression which would translate into Shakespearean English as "Et tu, Brute?"

The compartment of my mind, which was cracking silly jokes had to be switched off, as the gravity of the situation dawned on me. I was faced with a bunch of foreigners who were questioning my closely held beliefs. Frankly, I had never bothered to question this belief myself. In fact I was not a born meat-eater. I had not tasted meat till I was 28 years old. Of late I had been travelling a lot. Vegetarian food was available but one had to search really hard for it. Besides, my food choices started becoming a hindrance in socializing, building relationships with clients, colleagues and other business partners. I had decided to indulge in local food to whatever extent possible. I didn't mind eating chicken, duck etc. and quite relished fish and other seafood, be it chili crab in Singapore or fish head curry in Malaysia or Sashimi in Japan. But I had never even considered eating beef. When I was a pure vegetarian, the stories of snake eaters, dog eaters, rabbit eaters had really made me feel sick so I had drawn a line for myself at whatever flies or swims. But I could not have explained this to my current audience. If I had said this I would appear apologetic and unjustified. Most of them would go back to their countries thinking that Indians are not rational people. I could not lie, yet I had to come up with a convincing explanation. I had to do this by thinking rapidly on my feet.

"No. Bhagavd Gita doesn't explicitly" My belligerence continued.

There was a long pause, which I interpreted as, "Then why not be practical and start eating what the rest of the world eats?" But at the back of my mind, I was desperately trying to push back the effects of alcohol and reactivate the thinking compartment in my brain.

In the meanwhile, the question marks on their faces overflowed. Mr. Miller and Mr. Rahmat had mildly victorious expressions on their face. Mr. Park wanted to do something but the discussion went too fast for him to contribute. Kato-san wore his usual poker face.

At that moment, several things were running around randomly in my mind. My processor was going into uncharted regions in the brain to look for any possible data, sayings, or just anything, anything that would help me answer this question without evading it.

All I remembered was that my grandfather had told me – a cow has gods inside her stomach. Even at age 5, it did not make sense to me. But, I knew milk, which was my most favorite comfort food in childhood, came from a cow. Not just milk, I liked all the derived products like yogurt, buttermilk, butter and ghee.

When I visited my ancestral village, I saw dried cow-dung being used as fuel. I had heard my uncles say that cow-dung was one of the cheapest and best fertilizers available to them. During one such trip, I also saw a cow giving birth to a male calf, which later worked at the farm. The calf's birth was celebrated as if there had been a human birth in the house. The entire village visited us in the next few days to take a look at the newborn calf. The cow and the calf were a part of the family. I had heard my aunt talking to the cow softly and often seen her wiping her own tears. When I grew up I realized that this is called pet-therapy.

Against this backdrop, there was no way I would even consider eating beef. The cow was an integral part of the family. But none of these arguments would hold water against my audience in the by-lanes of Seoul, turning over high quality, marinated beef, which probably came from the distant cousin of my uncle's calf.

By this time, the first pieces of beef were ready. Mr. Miller, Kato-san, Mr. Rahmat and Mr. Park were busy eating and appreciating the beef. They appeared very pleased. They started turning over the next piece on the barbeque and refilling the soya sauce and other condiments.

My throat began to feel dry. I sipped green tea instead of rice wine. I felt better. Mr. Miller was talking to Mr. Rahmat about his past experience as a banker and I heard the word ROI for the umpteenth time from him.

There came the 'Eureka' moment. I don't know if it was the cocktail of rice wine and green tea that did the trick or if I had pushed my brain too hard or if there was a short-circuit between my left and right brain. But suddenly everything became very clear to me. The clouds of doubt had gone and open blue skies had returned.

"There are reasons," I threw my hat back into the ring.

"Excuse me? Did you say something?" asked Mr. Miller, who had celebrated his victory with a second piece of beef and was shocked to hear what he heard. His face was almost like that of a boxer who after knocking out his opponent is expecting the referee to declare him the winner and instead sees the opponent getting up and taking his stand again.

"There are tangible, logical reasons why Indians don't eat beef," everyone noticed the growing confidence in my voice. "....and what are these?" said Mr. Rahmat in a voice full of astonishment, curiosity laced with sarcasm. I ignored all of this and continued.

"Indian civilization started in what was known as the *Sapt-Sindhu* (Land of seven rivers) at least a thousand years before Christ," I had to ignore the resigned look of exasperation on Mr. Miller's face for having to listen to the obvious. Somehow, I had captured the attention of all the others with my opening sentence.

"Thanks to the abundance of water, fertile land and wisdom of a few good men, agriculture was invented. Ancient civilization quickly transformed from hunters into farmers. They soon improvised on the farming technology and realized that bulls were extremely helpful in farming. They also realized that the cow was a very useful animal. It gave milk, which was a great protein supplement. All the milk by-products quickly became an integral part of the diet. Cow dung assumed importance as fertilizer as well as fuel to burn traditional cooking '*Chullahs*' to cook. Most importantly, cows gave birth to bulls," I paused and gave a victorious smile to my audience, but they were still unimpressed.

So I continued my hard sell. "If you consider the by- products such as milk, fertilizer, fuel, leather and the number of bulls a cow can produce in her lifetime, the ROI - which is also known as return on investment" at this point I looked at Mr. Miller dead in the eye, "of a living cow is much better than that of a dead cow." I took a long pause and looked around, since I had made the most important point.

I had to ensure everyone was following me before I continued, "A few wise men at the top had realized this, but their challenge was to communicate this to the masses. How to make sure that everyone in the country stays away from the tasty meat? If the cows were reared for meat, the agriculture based society would not be sustainable. Therefore, they came up with an explanation, which the masses would accept without a doubt, at that time. They argued that the status of cow should be the same as status of one's mother since it is was a primary source of milk. They declared that killing a cow would be a heinous crime. Killing of cows stopped. People realized the conveniences and advantages of agriculture. The goal was accomplished." This came out much better than I had expected.

"As a rational thinking individual, I know that a cow cannot be a God but the benefits of the by-products and ROI generated from a living cow is undeniably higher than a dead cow." I completed my reasoning. I declared the end of my speech by sipping some green tea and looking at the audience to see if there were any questions.

"That makes sense," Kato-san was the first one to give in.

Mr. Park heaved a sigh of relief and winked at me with a smile on his face. "..better ROI, huh.. We never thought about it this way," Mr. Miller did not want to accept his defeat without protest. 'Hasta la vista baby', I said to myself in Arnold Schwarzenegger style and stashed my imaginary gun back in its holster. My seafood had arrived and I started to barbecue it.

The clincher I was looking for arrived in the nick of time. In automotive parlance we call it Just-In-Time (JIT).

The shape of the question marks on their faces changed. The new shape now meant, "Why the hell did I not think of this before?" Soon,

I had some friendly and appreciative faces around me. I am not sure if they agreed with everything I said but the argument could not be brushed away. I was convinced about it myself. I am not sure if this was the actual reason for denominating the cow as a God, but whatever I had said sounded perfectly logical to me. I had won my audience over with this impeccable argument. I patted my own back in my mind and started looking for the imaginary champagne bottle.

But it wasn't over yet. Mr. Rahmat definitely wasn't going to allow me to get off the hook so easily. I don't know if it was because he was feeling slightly ignored by Mr. Miller and Kato- san for a while or the discovery of strong logic in a seemingly meaningless concept or whether it was his genuine curiosity, but he opened another can of worms.

"That sounds pretty reasonable Mr. Vaidya," carefully avoiding the word 'logical', he pushed on, "but can you explain why so many Indians are vegetarians?"

"Vegetarians?" Mr. Miller wasn't exactly aware of this aspect. Mr. Rahmat took the center-stage with this much-required boost from Mr. Miller's genuine curiosity.

"Yes, of course! Many Indians are pure vegetarians. Forget beef, they won't even eat any meat!" Mr. Rahmat was beginning to sound irritated.

"Oh yes! Many of them don't even eat egg, you know," This was a new voice in the conversation. We all looked at who it was. Mr. Park could not sit on the fence anymore. I reckoned that being a conference organizer, he must have received the rough end of this stick. I was sure that some fellow countryman would have given him a tough time. I didn't have to wait too long to hear from the horse's mouth.

Mr. Park started narrating his experience with long pauses and an acquired American accent, "Last year we had an Indian speaker in our conference. He was so famous. Sponsor said they pay money only if he comes."

I realized that he was struggling with his grammar too. He was probably thinking in Korean and talking in English. The translation compartment in the brain had probably started getting traces of rice wine so it was not working at its best.

But Mr. Park pushed on, "..this fellow was so different. His first condition was that he should get vegetarian food only and he would not attend the welcome dinner even if they serve him vegetarian food because he can't stand the smell of non-vegetarian barbecue." I could quickly categorize my fellow countryman perhaps from down south, senior age group, infrequent traveler, religious Hindu and perhaps *Brahmin* by caste. After an hour or so in front of the beef barbecue, I had started sympathizing with this knowledgeable speaker. The smell of burning calf meat had filled the air, which made me uncomfortable.

"Then what happened? Did you get the food he wanted?" Mr. Rahmat wisely put some oil in the fire.

Mr. Park's face so far was quite grim and inexpressive till this discussion started. But the discussion about vegetarianism stimulated his expressiveness. With his eyebrows raised in amazement, a slight smile on his face and a bit of irritation in his voice, he continued, "We were very careful because he was the most important guest, you know! We ordered a vegetarian soup, bread and sautéed vegetables for his lunch. As soon as the lunch was served, he looked at it very suspiciously. Then he started smelling the food."

Mr. Rahmat broke into laughter. Mr. Miller also laughed loudly. Kato-san hid his lips behind a paper napkin. Realization that a formidable alliance was building up for even tougher quizzing ahead was slowly dawning upon me.

"Then he became very angry and called for the manager." "Really? The manager? Then?" said Mr. Rahmat

"He started asking the Manager whether it was vegetarian. The Manager said yes. But our guest was still not convinced. So the Manager called the chef. The Chef, very famous, Sir! was very angry when called like this," said Mr. Park. He was gathering immense sympathy. The Restaurant Manager served the next batch of beef pieces.

"What's the matter the chef asked. Then the manager say we tell him all dish vegetarian but he no agree," Mr. Park had officially given up any attempt to speak in grammatically correct English, as his thoughts outpaced his grammar processor.

"Of course, it is not all vegetarian dish. We make vegetable soup in chicken stock and use oyster sauce for sautéed vegetables."

I was about to shout in favor of the speaker brother from my country but when I looked around the mood was different. Nobody had caught the contradiction.

"So?" Mr. Miller asked.

"You know...Sir, they cannot even have soup made in chicken stock or oyster sauce."

"Really?"

"Yes Sir !"

The entire gathering except me was in positive feedback loop. Their surprise levels, excitement level and sarcasm levels were at an all-time high. I began to realize the potency of the alliance.

"So what did you do then?" Mr. Miller was looking for more astonishing facts about Indians to make his maiden interaction even more exciting.

"Well...," Mr. Park was controlling his laughter, "the chef offered to make cheese pasta in tomato sauce for him. I thank the chef for his presence of mind. He saved the day for us."

"What pasta?" roared Mr. Miller in an unusually loud voice.

"Cheese pasta..." Mr. Park was trying to figure out if he said something wrong.

"But if they can't eat meat, why are milk based products accepted? In the end, both are animal based products, right?" Mr. Miller's logical brain was live enough despite the intoxication to spot the contradiction.

I was still hoping that this newly formed hurricane would change its direction and go away rather than approach me. But Mr. Rahmat was not ready to let that happen. After all, he was the creator of this hurricane. He wanted to stay firmly in control of its direction.

"How do you explain this, Mr. Vaidya? Don't they realize that such finicky behavior may cause inconvenience to efficient organizers like Mr. Park? And isn't it completely illogical to accept milk and not accept meat when both are animal based products?" said Mr. Rahmat. Mr. Park held up his wine glass to accept the compliment and offered his silent but active support to Mr. Rahmat.

I found myself in a corner, once again. Some of these practices had a reason and rationale, some of them hadn't. Since they were an integral part of the Hindu religion, they were never really critically analyzed or reasoned out. But here I was, surrounded by a few foreigners, who were likely to form an opinion about my religion, my country and my people based on my answers in the next few minutes. In the earlier 'beef-debate,' I had nothing to lose. I casually built my argument. But now there was performance pressure. I switched back to my data search and synthesis mode.

Actually, not all Indians are vegetarians. Its only Hindus of *Brahmin* caste and followers of the Jain and Buddhist religions, who are generally vegetarians. I had read a survey, which put the percentage of non-vegetarians in India at 60-65%. So the odds of getting an Indian who is a staunch vegetarian was 1 in 3. But those who are vegetarians are staunch vegetarians. They would prefer to skip a meal or eat just fruits than eat meat. Usually, such staunch vegetarians belong to the *Brahmin* caste, or they are Jains, or belong to some sects of Buddhism. I knew the story till here and now I had to quickly build a reasonable explanation about why they behave like this and cause inconveniences to the likes of Mr. Park and others. My mind began to wander into things that we had learnt, read and understood in a very unstructured manner from the age of 5 to 15.

There are four main *'varnas'* in India and after thousands of years, many castes have evolved. The *varna* system is a complete misfit in the modern way of living but it is hard for Indians to wish it away. It is strongly ingrained in you as your genes. It shapes your social status, education, wealth and what was most relevant for me at that moment, food choices.

I navigated my mind back to the four main *varnas*: *Brahmin* (priests and teachers), *Kshatriya* (warriors), *Vaishyas* (traders) and *Shudras* (service providers). These *varnas* were originally designed to ensure that every village - the smallest dwelling unit in ancient India - was self-sufficient.

Shudras were supposed to provide all services such as cleaning, transport etc., *Vaishyas* manufactured and traded goods, earned money and paid taxes for the village economy to function smoothly. *Kshatriyas* were the powerful varna, they ruled, protected the villages or cities from attackers and took care of the security of the entire community. *Brahmins* became priests, learnt Sanskrit, taught people and took care of spirituality. They were supposed to think, meditate, and educate the masses.

Each of these *varnas* had an important role to perform and therefore needed to have a specific mindset. *Kshatriyas* for example could have a 'rajas' mindset, which allowed them to indulge in worldly pleasures. *Brahmins* on the other hand were supposed to have a *'satvik'* mindset which made them *shant* (pious), *sanyami* (control anger and other negative emotions) and *kshamasheel* (forgiving) people. They were not supposed to pursue wealth, yet in the social hierarchy they would occupy the highest level. They were worshipped and respected, even by kings. They were supposed to be selfless, and therefore their advice carried weight. They were supposed to occupy the highest moral ground and advise the masses on how to achieve nirvana or moksha (redemption).

I was completely lost in my thoughts and didn't notice which way the hurricane had gone. When I looked around, I felt quite ignored, as Mr. Miller was sharing a management joke and Mr. Park and Mr. Rahmat were laughing out loud. They were not expecting me to come up with a logical or reasonable answer anymore. 'Lightning doesn't strike twice in the same place,' they must have thought to themselves.

But after that power-meditation, I was not ready to concede defeat. I thought I still had a fighting chance to come up with a good explanation. I would have loved another 10 minutes to complete my thought process and build a solid argument but I sensed that time was running out. If Mr. Park proposed a couple of more '*Gonbaes*' nobody would be in a state of mind to understand the deep, logical explanation I was planning to unveil. I decided to go for it.

"Ahem ahem," I cleared my throat. Nobody except Kato- san noticed. Perhaps he was looking at me from behind his paper napkin covering his mouth and was probably hoping that I would come up with some explanation.

."...*aanoo*, baidya-san wants to say something," he called out to others.

I got the attention from a couple of surprised and irritated faces.

"The person who met Mr. Park, in all probability would be a *Brahmin*," I started confidently, although I could feel the imaginary wall behind my back. "What was his name?" asking questions is always a good breather and demonstrates your confidence.

"Mr. Gopalkrishnan," replied Mr. Park, "and he also had an orange vertical line on his forehead."

Bingo! I was right. He was a *Brahmin*.

"That's right, Mr. Park. He was indeed a *Brahmin*. An orange vertical line called *gandha* is their religious symbol." A few faces were in awe at my resurrection.

"*Brahmins* in the Hindu religion are the connection between God and the masses. They are supposed to be pious, forgiving people who do not pursue worldly pleasures. They are supposed to maintain the balance of society, forgive people, and keep the *Kshatriyas*, the powerful rulers, in check. They stand for peace. So how could they advocate violence against animals? How could they cause bloodshed even be it amongst animals? They didn't need the power and brute force that comes with eating meat. They believed that eating flesh and blood makes them aggressive, impatient and less forgiving, so they opted for food that does not have any flesh. They relied mostly on a plant-based diet, and had milk and milk-based products as protein supplements."

I looked around. Everyone was listening intently. These were theories they hadn't heard before. I was not sure they agreed with everything but at least they were listening, and wanted more of it.

"They developed an entire dietary system that was plant based. As I mentioned earlier, India had fertile land, a well- developed river system and it made tremendous sense to have a farming based society rather than a hunting based society. Those were the early days of civilization where animal farming was not yet invented. Farming itself was a break through invention that brought peace, stability and therefore prosperity to the masses. It naturally caught on and *Brahmins* practiced it to the core. Millennia have gone by, but a significant number of Indians still practice this. They still want to pursue that pious, controlled life that their ancestors adopted. For generations, this group of people have never eaten meat and therefore developed an aversion for it. They may not necessarily consider killing an animal a sin but they definitely consider it an avoidable activity which they can do away with."

I knew I was doing well but I was not sure if I could celebrate an imaginary victory as yet. There was a brief silence, the moment that is often described as angels passing by, where everyone was thinking and waiting for someone else to speak. But who would go first?

."...*aano*, I agree with Baidya-san," Kato-san emerged as a savior, a secret ally, "Vegetarianism is very very good. In Japan, in Okinawa prefecture, people live for many many years and many of them even cross 100 years. Okinawa diet is majorly plant based. They eat very less fish, less pork as compared to other Japanese. They say that more vegetarian, light weight diet helps them to live longer."

Long live Kato-san! I hoped that slogan shouting in my head was not audible to others. Kato-san had delivered a knockout punch. They had not thought about vegetarianism that deeply. They had never linked it to a long life. Everyone except Mr. Rahmat looked quite content and was probably bored with these quizzical discussions. Mr. Rahmat, still had something up his sleeve and I was quite curious to know what it was. If he argued too much he was going to make himself look bad. I got ready to field the next question.

"Mr. Vaidya, if I am not mistaken you are a *Brahmin* too. Then why are you eating that seafood?" Mr. Rahmat in his desperate attempt to score a goal was getting too personal. It was in some sense a very offensive question. But I took a deep breath, looked at my watch from corner of my eye, looked at the red-eyes of people sitting around.

I knew the dinnertime and allowable alcohol limit in the bloodstream for a hangover-free morning was hitting its limit. I sensed that it was not the time for a logical, sincere answer. What could be better than cracking a joke? My mind was itching to do it for a long time. The right time was probably now.

I pointed at Mr. Park and Daisy and said, "I became non- vegetarian to save them some trouble and to make sure that you guys don't hold any other Indian in a corner and ask him such difficult questions." I burst into laughter. All the others joined in. For the first time in the evening, we all saw how Kato-san's genuine smile looked. Mr. Park signaled something to the restaurant manager. She rushed in with a special bottle of red Korean wine and its special glasses. Mr. Park poured this special wine for everyone. Even in this semi-drunk state he did not pour for himself. I took the rest of the wine and poured it for him and Daisy. "Gonbae for successful conference tomorrow" we all shouted. There were many clinks, with smiling faces gulping down the special wine.

The conference the next day was a huge success. The bonding of all speakers and panelists was quite evident. Since then I have spoken at Mr. Park's conferences several times. Mr. Miller & Mr. Rahmat are very close professional acquaintances and my trip to Japan is never complete without meeting Kato-san.

Now if someone asks me why Indians are vegetarians, I smile and say, "to avoid bloodshed." They invariably ask why am I eating meat? I smile further and say, "So as to not cause you any trouble." Then when they control their irritation and ask me why I don't eat beef, I laugh loudly, wink and say, "ROI!"

2

WHY DO INDIANS GO FOR ARRANGED MARRIAGE?

Marrakesh is a small, sleepy town in Morocco, with a long history. The absence of skyscrapers and high-rises contributes to a harmonious appearance and shifts the focus to the royal mosque with its tall minaret that can be spotted from anywhere. While the snow-capped mountain range, not too far from the town, helps fight the fiery heat of the sun, the inherent warmth and friendliness of the locals makes it very easy for everyone to feel comfortable. Friendly, happy and smiling people obviously spot you as a foreigner but greet you to make you feel at home. The wide and clean street walks are lined with orange trees. The oranges hanging from the trees in the summer season remind you that you are at an exotic location.

My wife Nalini and I were walking on these sidewalks hand in hand as a caravan of horse drawn carriages passed by. We were in Marrakesh for a conference, which had just ended, and we were walking back from a local restaurant after dinner. Soon we were in the Souk area, the busiest and noisiest but the most fun part of the town.

Everyone converges on the Souk area as the sun sets and the market place comes alive. Hundreds of shopkeepers try to persuade you rather aggressively to shop. You have to make your way through haggling shoppers. Often it is difficult to say which is more fun, shopping or haggling.

As we were drifting slowly across, smiling to ourselves, a teenage girl wearing the traditional headscarf held my wife's hand and started making a henna tattoo on it. Nalini pulled her hand back in a natural reflex action and asked the girl to go. But the henna girl was very persuasive. She offered to draw a small design free of cost, which of course was a marketing gimmick. She was quite skilled, so we were drawn into watching her artistic hand movements and beautiful design. Soon she drew her henna design all over Nalini's left hand.

"50 dirhams, please," the girl demanded. "What?" I got into the haggler's role-play.

"Sir, we live on this. Things have become so expensive. 50 dirhams is nothing for you."

It is difficult to haggle with women. They take you on an emotional path. I was looking for my next best argument when Nalini pulled out 50 dirhams from her purse and gave it to the henna girl with a smile. She thanked us profusely. Nalini pulled me away from the crowd and soon we were walking on a much less crowded street.

Nalini admired the quick henna art on her left hand and said, "I never got a chance to apply henna after our wedding." Women have an advanced database management algorithm that can retrieve any time-date-location-related memory in a flash.

"Yeah, that's true! You never got a chance," I pretended as if I remembered this.

"Just look at it. What do you see?" She looked into my eyes as she said this.

Women are very smart, they can easily call your bluff, I thought. Maybe she realized that I didn't remember anything about the henna and she was challenging me. My heart sank. I was looking forward to a romantic walk back but this unplanned 'Who Wants To Be A Millionaire' episode without any help lines, was about to spoil my plans. But having said what I had said, I had no other choice but to face the situation. I held her hand and pretended to observe the henna painting deeply, turning her palm a little bit to get a good look.

Frankly, most of these henna drawings look the same to me. They are nice and intricate but similar. Round and round.. dots here and there.. As I inspected her palm without saying anything, I could feel the expectations rising and my heart sank further.

"Do you remember something?" her curiosity was peaking.

I couldn't think of anything, I closed my eyes, kissed good- bye to the idea of a romantic walk and said, "It looks familiar. Very similar to a design that I have seen before."

Actually, I wanted to say it looked similar to every design that I have seen before, but I had to put it in a politically correct manner. I was readying myself for the next level of questions with increasing difficulty but suddenly, Nalini hugged me and whispered, "I love you so much."

What!!! I couldn't believe it. Did I just hit a bull's eye? But how??

"It's not allowed in this country," I rescued myself from her hug and murmured.

But she was all upbeat, "I don't care! You really surprised me. You remembered that I had a very similar henna design on our wedding day."

I couldn't believe my luck. It's not everyday that you shoot an arrow in the dark and hit a bull's eye. I looked up and thanked my stars and put on a facial expression, which said, "Yeah baby! I know I am the best."

But I really wonder why women feel all romantic when the men in their lives remember trivial details of the past. If I didn't remember the exact design of the elaborate henna which adorned her hands on our wedding day that didn't make me a bad husband. Then why do they test men's memory all the time?

But for now, I brushed those things aside and returned to the situation, which was increasingly turning in my favor.

She held my hand firmer, walked closer and said, "The moon looks so romantic…"

"Yeah! It does" I looked up and it didn't look any different from it usually does to me but I had to build the romantic mood further.

So I said, "The moon reminds me of a romantic song." She looked at me with surprise. Her big eyes and bow shaped eyebrows looked absolutely kissable.

Then I hummed Mohammad Rafi's "khoya khoya chand" as we walked along the sidewalk in a completely unknown land amongst a few curious onlookers. It was really very romantic.

"You had sung this song when we were walking back to our cottage in coorg." Any romantic memory is incomplete without the time-date-location stamp.

"Of course!" I patted her head which she had just rested on my shoulder, as we were walking into our hotel, mentally exiting the city with rules against public displays of affection.

As I was excitedly swiping the card to get into the room, I heard her yawning as she said, "I am so tired. I want to crash into bed."

"Are you sure?" I meant I felt very fresh and energized.

We had been married for 15 years and Nalini is a very intelligent woman so she easily spotted where this conversation was headed.

"Absolutely. It was you who promised to take your dear boss to Casablanca tomorrow and because of that, we need to get up early in the morning."

I learnt two important things. One: a time-date stamp doesn't just figure in romantic discussions but women can very effectively use it to put any argument to rest. Two: Romantic feelings in Indian marriages are quite short lived, and unlike Hollywood movies they often lead nowhere.

In this case, like in most cases, she was right. Due to connecting flight problems, we had a free day in Morocco. I had figured out that the world's second largest mosque was in Casablanca, which was a couple of hours drive from Marrakesh, and I wanted to go there. My boss liked the idea and said that he and his wife would join us. So going to bed immediately was the only option.

Next morning, a Mercedes van came to pick us up. In the cabin there were spacious seats where both couples could sit comfortably facing each other. My boss Alan was British and lived in London. He has a plumpish frame, is tall, and is well over fifty. Since I work in Singapore, I hardly got a chance to meet him face to face for months, and this was the first time I was meeting his wife.

Samantha was a blonde woman, almost as tall as Alan, with shoulder length hair, and she wore a pair of branded sunglasses over her hair. Age had altered the colour of her hair and left some creases around her eyes and smile lines. She was wearing a black, polka dotted full-sleeved top with white trousers. Alan was his enthusiastic self in a denim jeans and T-shirt which had multi-colored horizontal lines that did not suit his plumpish body frame. I guess all corporate workers get bored of wearing blue and grey for the entire week and hence want to make up for all of it on weekends and vacations.

I greeted Alan with a firm handshake and did the same for Samantha. But she moved her face towards me. I had seen others doing the cheek-kiss ritual but it was my first time that too under the watchful eyes of my better half. Needless to say I was very clumsy. It felt pretty tricky to me, you hug but don't touch, kiss but don't kiss, and have momentary intimacy. After fumbling with the cheek kiss on the right side we had to go on to the left but I aborted the operation. There was an awkward moment but that was better than a clumsy kiss. I sincerely think there must be a visionary perfume company behind promoting this ritual and keeping it alive. Samantha's perfume smelled expensive, I wished I had used mine and gotten up five minutes earlier to shave. Damn!

After watching our cheek-kiss fiasco, Nalini folded her hands to do the Namaste gesture to Alan, who had extended his hand for a handshake. Seeing Nalini doing the Namaste, he too folded his hands, as Nalini extended her hand for a handshake. They got stuck in a loop of alternate *namaste*s and handshakes. After a couple of iterations, they gave up. It was obvious we came from different worlds. But we all laughed loudly and it was all okay in the end.

I went to instruct the van driver about our itinerary, enquire about travel time etc. and as Alan and Samantha got in, Nalini hung around outside the van awkwardly. Alan and Samantha occupied the last row leaving the row facing them for us. We started our day-long trip to Casablanca to see the world's second largest mosque. Little did I know that it would be a journey into the Indian marriage system.

As we started driving, Alan started looking out of the window to check out the scene, Nalini was looking at her toes, Samantha was looking at Nalini and I was all confused about how to get the conversation going. Samantha sensed the awkward silence and came up with a genuine icebreaker.

"Your henna design looks pretty good," she said. Overnight the henna had turned from a muddy brown color to an orange red color. In India, they say if a husband loves his wife then the henna turns into a darker color. By that yard stick, we were couple in love.

"Thanks!" Nalini smiled genuinely to accept the compliment and offered her hand to Samantha for a closer look.

Then the two ladies started discussing different elements of the designs, which I had broadly classified as curves, in detail. For women it's not enough to say that I like the entire design. It is essential to appreciate all the smaller elements.

"You draw henna designs during your weddings, right?" Samantha had attended my colleague's wedding in Punjab and I had heard she had had a ball of a time a few years ago. She managed to strike the right chord with Nalini.

"Yeah! This is the first time I got to apply henna after our wedding."

"Really. That's so sweet!" Samantha also got excited and said, "Tell me more."

It's quite amusing to see two women talk. They use words like "sweet" and "cute" which don't really fit in but both of them seem to understand or at least pretend that they understand. For a woman, an enthusiastic, willing listener who is interested in all the possible details creates more excitement than sex, perhaps.

I was happy that we were getting along well after the cheek- kiss fiasco. Alan knew where the conversation was headed, so he started to admire the scenery around us. The decibel levels of woman folk reached a peak Nalini said, "Yeah, and can you believe this design is very similar to what I had at the time of my wedding."

"How long were you dating before you got married?" It seemed like Samantha wanted to have a genuinely long conversation with us.

Nalini and I looked at each other. If a woman looks at you, you should safely assume that she wants you to take the lead in the situation. We got married in a traditional arranged way. Nalini was not sure whether we wanted to talk about that with Samantha and Alan.

"About a month. Ours was an arranged marriage," I said.

Samantha was completely surprised. Probably, she had heard about Indian arranged marriages but had never met someone who had actually done it. Perhaps, she had a completely different mental image of an arranged married couple Maybe she had many wrong notions about this system. In any case, the conversation had taken a decisive turn and was now more than skindeep.

Samantha leaned forward, part of her palm touching her chin, extended forefinger on her cheek, a classic pose indicating a high level of interest and curiosity. Alan on the other hand, pretended as if he hadn't heard us, pulled out his iPad and Blue tooth ear set and started to watch videos. It was quite odd that he had the headset that covered only his left ear leaving the right ear open – which I guessed was to listen to us. But he pretended to be busy and disinterested in our discussion. I couldn't escape like Alan, I knew Nalini would expect me to be by her side. After all, I had opened the can of worms.

I glanced outside. The drive was beautiful. Marrakesh to Casablanca was about two hundred and thirty kilometers, which we expected to cover in two hours and thirty minutes. Green colour dominated the scene up to the horizon. There were cattle and sheep grazing merrily. The farmers had cleverly used tall cactus plants to fence in the cattle. Every single thing visible outside was relaxing and pleasing, and I was eager to absorb every bit of it. Except now, I was going to be involved in discussions around our arranged marriage.

I have had this experience many times. There are so many misconceptions around arranged marriages that you don't know where to start and where to end. So since most time I tend to avoid the discussions, I thought, "Maybe today is the day I should face it."

"So, how does this work? Let me guess, you guys saw each other just before the wedding, since your parents had already made the decision, right?" Samantha was trying to put forth what she had heard, in a nice and friendly manner. That's what she must have thought, but we didn't find it friendly enough.

"That's history, Samantha. It probably used to happen when our parents got married. Now, the girl and the boy are consulted well before the decision is made," I tried to put up a brave face and add a modern tinge to this age-old tradition.

"Consulted?" Samantha burst into laughter, "That's very interesting," she immediately said, trying to control herself. Perhaps, she meant that it's pathetic and that we should be the ones to decide and no one else.

Nalini pitched in, "But in our case, we made the decision ourselves and informed our parents."

"Really?" Quintessential sarcasm peeped from her tone, "That's great. How does that work?"

Nalini continued innocently, "Our parents got in touch with each other through a common friend. They exchanged our horoscopes, and they matched perfectly! 100 out of 100, can you believe it?" Nalini held my hand as she said this, not realizing that she was walking into an argument trap.

"Wow, that's awesome," Samantha said without a hint of emotion.

"Do you guys still believe in horoscope matching? Isn't it insane to think that stars and planets which are millions of kilometers away can predict whether two people are compatible?" Samantha's argument was logically correct but it was a little too direct. We looked at each other. Actually, both of us didn't believe in this horoscope thing. We had done it for the sake of our respective parents. We had talked about it and joked about it. But now we needed a strong argument.

"Have you read Linda Goodman's Sun Signs?"

"Yes. I like that book. It predicts mine and Alan's nature perfectly," Samantha said, unknowingly.

"Just as you read Sun Signs, you like it but don't take it too seriously, it's the same with horoscopes," I battled on, "We got married to each other because we liked each other. Horoscopes were just something that our parents wanted to do."

"Parents?"

"Yes. It is very important to have the blessings of our parents and families before we get married," Nalini added.

"But why? Why do parents have such a big say when it's about two people who want to live with each other for rest of their lives?" Samantha asked. Now I noticed that her initial emotional reactions and sarcasm had given way to genuine curiosity.

Samantha's question was quite valid. We had not thought about it. So Nalini started describing our wedding ceremony, "Not just the marriage decision; our parents, brothers, sisters were involved at every step in the wedding ceremony. Both he and I had to complete the morning rituals with our parents, then after a particular ritual we were declared married. All rituals after that were done together. For some specific rituals, they needed my brother and his sister."

I also butted in, "Although, I don't remember all the rituals, the last ritual is clearly etched in my mind. The priest made me and Nalini sit in the center, my parents on the side, followed by my siblings and all my uncles, aunts, grandparents, the entire extended family. Then he asked everyone to give their blessings to the married couple as a family - which symbolized the acceptance of the bride into the family, with the promise that everyone would be responsible for her welfare. Our marriage in short involved the entire family."

I added, "In contrast, my colleague Tina's marriage looked completely different. The bride's father escorted her to the dais and then the groom took over. Then onwards it was the couple's show. We didn't even feel the presence of either parents in the entire ceremony."

Samantha was quite impressed to notice the contrast. She said, "Now I get it. In Indian marriages, it's not just the couple that gets married, its two families that get married."

"Exactly," Nalini looked visibly happy, "The tradition is that the entire family should wholeheartedly accept the other family for a lasting marriage. This cross-family bond ensures that everyone supports the couple in good times and bad times. Should something go wrong between the couple..." Nalini skillfully avoided the word 'divorce', "the entire family works together to make sure the marriage is successful."

"Hmm. That's an interesting perspective. Does this happen in love marriages too?"

This was easy - both of us had just read the book '2 States' by Chetan Bhagat.

"Yes. Of course," Nalini said cheerfully, "In love marriages, the boy likes the girl. The girl likes the boy and then they decide to get married. But then the girl needs to convince her family and the boy needs to convince his family too. Then the families meet, the boy's family should like the girl and the girl's family should like the boy and then the girl's family should like the boy's family and the boy's family should like the girl's family. Then, they can get married."

Nalini was too engrossed in her argument, so she didn't notice how many 'likes' she had created. Samantha and I smiled a bit.

"Basically, the difference between love marriage and arranged marriage is only up to the point both families accept the relationship.

That is an essential step for a long happy marriage, even in a love marriage. I have seen so many love marriages which didn't have familial blessings, perish" Nalini summarized.

"This way of getting married seems a bit complex but it creates a strong foundation for a long lasting relationship. The divorce rate in India is quite low," I took the argument to statistics - my area of comfort, "As per the latest survey of population, it is less than 10 percent of the entire population."

"That's pretty low," Samantha accepted. But she still looked unconvinced.

"But... What about love? What about romance? What about likeability? What about sexual compatibility? Isn't all this very important? What if the two don't click?"

She had a valid point. We know many couples around us who hadn't clicked. We were lucky, we did. All of them may not get divorced necessarily, but just keep pulling along. The divorce rates are quite understated.

Sex before marriage is a 'No-No' in Indian arranged marriages. Sexual compatibility of the couple is taken for granted.

"All of these are very important, but Indian girls look for commitment more than anything else. Even if my husband is not macho, nor handsome it is okay, but I want him to be committed." Nalini came in with a gem of a thought.

"When the boy woos a girl, he puts on his best behavior and persona. He tries hard to impress the girl and win her heart. Once that is done, slowly the romance evaporates. Unseen problems start to appear and things are not warm and mushy anymore," Nalini was on a roll.

"In our case, it was a thought through decision. We were aware of all our problems and expectations from each other. So we were better prepared to make this marriage successful," Nalini completed her statement and held my hand for moral support.

"Yeah. That is true. Commitment is no doubt important for long-term relationships. But how can you have it before romance? How can you feel committed towards a person you don't feel much for?"

"In Indian arranged marriages, romance and love follow commitment," I said

"What if it doesn't?" Samantha asked, "In love marriages, the couple is in love, so commitment follows."

We didn't have an answer. Maybe we were conditioned to be committed since childhood. Maybe this was the only way we saw it happen. Maybe we had seen a lot of resistance to love marriages in the past and ultimately they were not as magical as they promised to be. In our case, we had a month long courtship before we got married. We were quite a romantic couple, so much so that some of our friends refused to believe that ours was an arranged marriage. But Samantha had a point and we did not have an answer.

"And what if commitment does not follow love?" To our surprise Alan joined the conversation. I knew he was listening to us. But this was unexpected. Samantha gasped, she struggled for words. She murmured something like, "it usually does follow... but yeah it is not necessary," or something like that.

"Maybe I can answer this," Alan offered to answer.

"I was watching a TED talk 'The Brain in Love' by Helen Fischer, and some of her points answers your question." Alan was a great orator and could hold any audience spellbound if he had a good story to tell. He started summarizing what he had heard on TED.

"As a human being we are born to reproduce and propagate the species. To accomplish this, our brain has developed three distinct centers of attraction. There is one center that is triggered by lust. It makes us want to have a partner. This center creates the need. The other center creates the romantic love in our minds. This is a special feeling that makes us stick to the selected partner, that makes us feel that the selected partner is the best possible choice, thus making us stick around with the partner long enough to produce an offspring. Romantic love is a unique feeling that has developed among human beings as a mating strategy. But it exists for a purpose. It is a means to an end. The end goal is successful procreation and nurturing of the next generation. It is by design a transient feeling."

I did not know that he was so good at non-managerial talks also.

"The center in the brain that deals with commitment is altogether a different center. It is not directly connected to lust or love. So theoretically, you can feel committed to a person without lust or love and you can feel lust or love towards a person without commitment," He paused.

"This is very interesting," said Samantha. "In a love marriage, the romantic love happens first, that forms the foundation of marriage, which lends itself to commitment. In an arranged marriage, the vow of commitment comes first and forms the foundation of marriage. Love marriage and arranged marriage are two alternate ways to a happy married life."

Alan continued, "Marriage is a completely artificial system we have overlaid on our animal brains. They are constantly working at cross purposes. By raw animal instinct, men are designed to give their sperm to as many women as possible and women are designed to look for the best possible sperm to give them great offspring, and they look for a man who would stick around with her during pregnancy and child birth. So commitment to stick around is very important for women. But left unregulated, these instincts must have caused chaos for society. So someone came up with the concept of marriage, and without exception every region and race advocates marriage for life. It forms the basic foundation of orderliness in society. Ultimately, how you got married has little to do with how long your marriage lasts or how happy it is."

His oratory rubbed off on me, "Exactly! Arranged marriage may not be an ideal system but in India it is thriving and it works. It not only ensures long lasting marriages but also ensures those who want to get married are not left behind. This age old system has adapted very well to the Internet too. There are various web portals that provide comprehensive services for self-arranged marriages. This is a bit like dating sites that we see in the Western world but with the ultimate aim of getting married, rather than just dating. In this system, commitment comes first and romance comes later; unlike in a love marriage where romance comes first and commitment later."

From the corner of my eye I glanced out and realized that we were approaching Casablanca, and I had to summarize this to ensure friendlier conversations on our return journey.

"The risk in an arranged marriage is that commitment may not lend itself to romance Just as in a love marriage, romance may not lead to commitment. For a successful marriage both romance and commitment are required. So does it really matter which comes first?"

At this point, the van driver interrupted our discussions and asked, "Should we see old Medina first or Hassan II mosque first?"

In the same breath I replied, "For a successful trip we need to see them both. Does it really matter which one we see first?" We all laughed. Nalini sent an invisible kiss to me through her eyes. I felt I am the luckiest man in the whole world!

3

WHY ARE INDIANS CRAZY ABOUT MOVIES?

I can safely say that taking care of a curious, extroverted and talkative foreigner in India, is one of the most difficult jobs in the world. Things become even more complicated if the person has come from the developed world for the first time, has read cultural sensitivity books about India and is also your client. Apart from the job they have to accomplish they are looking for some astonishing stories, some spicy gossip and extraordinary experiences, which they can go back and share with their folks.

They use words like "explore" or "discover" rather than "visit" India. Almost anything that is slightly different is an experience or adventure for them. It may be as trivial as eating at a roadside joint, or drinking tap water, or crossing a busy road. They are perpetually in the 'explore mode'. I feel like shouting at the top of my voice, "Dear friend, India by now is fully explored.

We have been living here for thousands of years, long before the countries you came from were populated. So technically you can't explore anything. If you want to know something, just ask!"

But I can't say any of this if the guest is my client or someone to whom I am supposed to show Indian culture, respect and tolerance. They notice and ask questions about many things that you have learnt to ignore from the age of five. They demand logical answers and explanations. It is often a losing battle. If you explain, they may find faults with your logic. If you don't, they may dismiss you. I hate to be in either situation. But this time, I had simply no choice.

I was taking care of an important client who had come from Germany for the first time to India. He had been sufficiently warned about the hazards and situations that he might face in India. He was armed with a Lonely Planet guide in German, a German-to-Hindi dictionary and an Evian water bottle. He appeared to have been coached by someone, whom we shall call his 'Explore India' Consultant.

It was the year 2010 and we were in Bangalore in an Ambassador taxi, which was moving at an average speed of eight kilometers per hour amidst lots of noise, the chief creator of which was driving our taxi. My guest, Mr. Schmidt, was a tall, thin-framed, bald gentleman, who had a permanent frown on his face. Even if he smiled whole-heartedly, the frown would not vanish, confusing the onlookers about his real feelings. Whatever he said with that expression sounded sarcastic, and I was not sure how I was going to take it for the next three days. We had not even reached Devanahalli from Bangalore's new airport and I was already feeling tired and fatigued by the situation I was in.

Our taxi driver honked loudly for the thirty-eighth time in the last thirty minutes or four kilometers. This was his way of inducing some sense of urgency into the traffic ahead as the lights turned green. This is a common practice in all major Indian cities. Motorists first press their horns instead of their accelerators when the traffic light turns green, which they genuinely believe causes the traffic to move ahead.

As they honk, the traffic starts to move and everyone in the traffic gets a temporary sense of achievement. Personally, I denounce this practice.

But it became very hard when my guest out of genuine curiosity asked, "why is the driver honking?" I looked outside the window pretending that I didn't hear the question. There was so much noise around that I got benefit of the doubt. My guest turned restless. Maybe this was one of the many questions he was seeking answers to and he had to do something to get the answers.

So he took out his dictionary and started constructing his first Hindi sentence. "*Aap...... bhopu.... jyada..... kyon.... baja..... raha....ho?*" he said to the driver. I had seen the dictionary but I never thought he would use it so soon. I had started sensing his urge to explore India. I was happy that he was dealing with the taxi driver directly, without my intervention. Manjunath, the driver, was a dark, well-built man sporting a thick mustache. He was petrified that a white man had spoken to him, and that too in Hindi! He took his eyes off the road, completely turned around to look at Mr. Schmidt who was sitting diagonally opposite the driver's seat. This in turn petrified Mr. Schmidt who could not even shout properly. I could no longer pretend that I was not there, as both my co-travelers were petrified for no apparent reason, one of them would be responsible for my career progression and the other for my life.

Before I could attempt to do anything, the car traveling to our left honked loudly to avoid a collision and our driver started looking at the road again. Mr. Schmidt took a sip out of his Evian bottle, while wiping the sweat on his bald head. Manjunath started talking to me in Kannada," *Sahebaru, yen helta idare, saar? Namage Hindi yenu barralla saar.*" (What is this respected man saying? I don't know Hindi at all.)

By 2010, I had stayed in Bangalore for 13 years. I had seen the transformation of this well planned, beautiful but sleepy city into India's premier IT hub. Knowledge workers, like me, from all over the country had made it their new home, but the local working class was found literally napping. Most of the population in Bangalore was well to do and the working class came from surrounding villages. Manjunath must be one of them. They were yet to discover compelling reasons to learn Hindi, so they mostly relied on Kannada and English, which pretty much sounded like Kannada. I had lived in Bangalore long enough and yet not found my own compelling reason to learn Kannada. I could only speak in broken Kannada, which I had learned without any formal training.

I said, "*Yen ree saar! English barata?*" (What is this? Do you know English at least?) I was trying to secure some lines of communication with Manjunath, as I couldn't trust my own Kannada skills.

In Bangalore, if you can speak Kannada with the local accent, they pardon the shortcomings in your grammar. Also calling each other "sir," pronounced as "*saar,*" is an integral part of Kannada spoken with non-Kannadigas.

"*Swalpa swalpa baratte saar. Sahebaru yaake namjote mataadatedare. Yen beka avarige? Nivu heli!*" (I know English but I don't feel confident talking to him. You know everything, it's better you talk to him.)

I could no longer run away from the situation. I informed Mr. Schmidt that the driver couldn't speak Hindi and though he understood English, he was not confident enough to speak to a white man. So he preferred to converse through me. I cut out all my own escape routes myself. Mr. Schmidt was amazed to hear that this supposedly uneducated man who didn't even know his own national language, knew English. He held his dictionary in his right hand and raised his eyebrows as if he was asking, "What am I supposed to do with this?"

"Why are you asking me? Go and ask your Explore India Consultant," I said inside my brain.

Outwardly, I just smiled and reassured him that the dictionary would be very useful in New Delhi, the next leg of his trip, where people speak Hindi and are scared to speak in English.

He was reassured but disappointed, and while putting the dictionary back into his luggage, must have made a mental note of the feedback he ought to give to his Explore India Consultant.

"Ask him why is he honking so much," said Mr. Schmidt. He didn't want to scare Manjunath any more, nor did he want to test his driving skills while looking at the rear seat.

"*Nivve heli saar. Nimage yalla gottu. Namage drive mad bekualwa?*" Said Manjunath as he honked at a big pothole right ahead.

This was directed towards me, and he meant that I should field such stupid questions and let him do his work. I was very irritated with the situation, with the excessive honking and me having to come up with a plausible explanation of these habits.

"Have you heard of vehicle-to-vehicle communication?" I decided to go overboard and nip this discussion in the bud. Mr. Schmidt nodded in the affirmative.

"This is the Indian version of that. It's called driver- to-driver communication. They are communicating through honking. If you notice carefully, he is using different sounds to communicate different things," I was hoping that Mr. Schmidt would start observing what the driver was doing and leave me alone for a while. But Mr. Schmidt asked his next question in less than seven minutes.

"Nobody is following any lane discipline. Those who want to make a right turn seem to be going in the left lane before making a right turn!" he said.

"Exactly," I had started to sound upbeat, "In our official meetings, we look at a person's body language and predict what he is likely to do, right? Similarly, a skilled driver can look at a vehicle's body language and predict where he is likely to turn next."

I wanted to say that 99% Indian drivers fall in this category, but then my argument would have sounded obvious or too smart to believe. Mr. Schmidt started observing more and realized that honking in India is not a discretionary activity, it is regarded as an essential one. The horn is not a sound creating feature, but a safety feature and driver-to-driver communication feature, rolled into one. A short honk while passing a car, for instance, is equivalent to "thanks buddy for letting me go through," whereas a loud, long honk is equivalent to "Hey guys, start moving! What the hell are you up to?"

After decoding the secret code of Indian honking, Mr. Schmidt turned his attention to the stray animals roaming around freely in the traffic. Mr. Schmidt was an informed man; his Explore India Consultant had warned him that he might see animals on the road, so he was not surprised to see them at all. In fact, he was expecting to see them. One more experience completed, some more India explored, he must have mentally ticked something off. But that did not deter him from asking me more questions.

He saw some stray dogs roaming around and fired his next salvo.

"Are these stray dogs sterilized?" "No."

"Then?"

"Then what?"

"Then how do you protect yourself from them?"

"Oh! Don't worry, they are not dangerous. They are quite domesticated. They are pets of the whole neighborhood," I said.

Much later in my life, I learnt that foreigners in India start worrying when they hear Indians saying "Don't worry." To foreigners this means that there is something that has been overlooked and the Indian accompanying them is going to think on his feet and would come up with a solution that is suboptimal. Indians call it '*jugaad*' but foreigners don't know this word. For foreigners "Don't worry" is a signal that things may start going downhill from there. Back then I was idyllically oblivious to their mental process and was happy that I had reassured my guest.

"Who picks their poo?" During those days I was also not exposed to pet care in developed countries. Those days I had no idea that in developed countries you need to move around with your pet with equipment to pick up the droppings. So obviously I was completely puzzled by the question.

"Government!" I answered confidently.

"Government? Really? How can they possibly manage that?" He gave me a look which clearly meant, "Don't try to pull my leg, I know this can't be true."

On the other hand I was thinking that he was pulling my leg. Who else could possibly pick up dog, (or for that matter all the other animal kingdom's) droppings?

"Why not? I mean, it's their duty to keep the roads clean, isn't it?" I stated the obvious reality.

Such conversations between foreigners and Indians are based on mutual disrespect. Both parties think that the other party is a fool, that they can't understand something so obvious and basic. The fact is, what is obvious and basic in one country is unimaginable in the other. Back then I was blissfully unaware of all this and kept pushing my argument.

Mr. Schmidt looked outside. It was quite obvious that government hadn't done its duty of cleaning anything for quite sometime. But my show of defiance didn't leave him with any choice.

"I must say the Indian government is the best for dog owners around the world!!" Mr. Schmidt turned sarcastic. I didn't understand why, so I ignored his remark.

"Who walks them?" Mr. Schmidt really wanted to get to the bottom of this.

I felt like laughing out loud but I controlled my instinct and just pointed out of the window. A gang war had erupted among some dogs, a few of them started barking loudly and chasing dogs from the other neighborhoods through the traffic, walking people, potholes and street vendors. The dogs were as much a part of the ecosystem as people were. A few men walking on the street, made way for the running dogs and cursed them at the same time. Seven to nine angry, barking dogs running at top speed through a sea of walking people is not a sight for fickle minded observer forget about Mr. Schmidt who had not even completed one hour on Indian soil. He took out his Evian and took another sip as he observed the dogs disappearing into the crowd. He must have downgraded "walking on Indian roads" to his not-to-do list. He also forgot all further questions about dogs.

I enjoyed a few moments of peace but Mr. Schmidt was observing a rather large cow standing at the corner of the road. Mr. Schmidt fumbled with his camera - those days mobiles with cameras were not so common - to take a picture. He seemed quite happy about the picture. Manjunath saw this from the corner of his eye and tried to suppress his chuckle, and I just looked out of the other window.

"Who feeds the cow?" Mr. Schmidt asked me.

Such a question had never occurred to me. People living in the developed world have exaggerated notions about their role in the world and life of animals in their care in particular. They tend to forget that every animal except for human beings, is perfectly capable of feeding itself, under even the most adverse conditions, as long as it is free to roam around. Only lazy human beings can't seem to do it. If you let your animal roam free, there is no need to walk the animal or even feed it.

"There is no need to feed the cow. It feeds itself."

Mr. Schmidt looked at me in disbelief. He thought I hadn't understood the question. So he started again.

"This cow belongs to someone, right?"

"Right."

"The owner protects the cow and milks her, right?"

"Right."

"So doesn't he feed her?"

"No."

Again the same look, with more irritation.

"Well, the owner just lets the cow roam free and the cow finds the food for itself," I said with a straight face.

Luckily, as I said this, we saw another cow grazing happily on the roadside grass. I pointed towards the cow. Mr. Schmidt fumbled with his camera again and took another picture. Another mental tick on his Explore India to-do list.

Manjunath understood what was happening. He said, "*Saar average heli kaleda tinglu aane banddithu, BTM layout alli.*" He wanted me to tell Mr. Schmidt that last month, some wild elephants had strayed into a locality called BTM layout on the outskirts of Bangalore.

"What is he saying?" Mr. Schmidt asked.

"We are about to reach our hotel," I said, to draw a curtain on discussions about the coexistence of Indians with their animals. Soon, we reached the hotel – The Windsor Manor.

The Windsor Manor, built in colonial style architecture, has a regal look to it. The entrance is through a bridge that is built only for patrons of the hotel. The interiors are designed to retain the colonial nostalgia with no compromise on modern day comforts. Right from the bellboy to the manager, every one seemed to know Mr. Schmidt's name. They welcomed him with a garland and a traditional ceremony using vermilion paste. The hotel had asked me if I wanted traditional music on the *mrudangam*, but I had declined. Mr. Schmidt was totally impressed. I thanked the hotel in my mind as they finally brought a smile on Mr. Schmidt's face.

The next couple of days were packed with official meetings. We were meeting Indian companies for breakfast, lunch and dinner. We were traveling in their cars and discussing business all the time. Mr. Schmidt had a very strong work ethic. He would always be on time for every meeting, and be focused fully on every discussion. We had no time for the cows, dogs and goats on the road, or speed breakers, potholes and honking among other things.

I thought I was going to escape this ordeal relatively unscathed, but Mr. Schmidt had other plans. We had wound up all the meetings, and we were traveling back to the Windsor Manor, tired out. The next day was deliberately kept free on Mr. Schmidt's request. Little did I know that this day was earmarked for "exploring" India. Considering my first encounter with him on the first day, I didn't dare to ask him what he wanted to do.

We went for dinner, just the two of us, in the Dakshin restaurant in Windsor Manor. It had a nicely spread out buffet which was a combination of Indian, East Asian and European cuisine. This restaurant has a glass roof, which could be opened on special occasions. We were sitting next to a well-illuminated swimming pool. After two days of busy schedules and highly successful meetings, I wanted to loosen up and enjoy my favorite dishes. In India, a buffet spread is just to let you know what is available. You could order each of those things especially for yourself, prepared fresh and customized to your taste. I had picked some *paneer* and chicken and ordered fresh *rotis*.

"Ah, Indian curries" said Mr. Schmidt, as he filled his dinner plate with salads, some pasta and bread.

"Indians don't like to call these things curries, please. Each dish is different and has completely different ingredients and method of preparation. Only those who don't know much about India call them curries." I scored a brownie point over his Explore India Consultant, who had failed to provide him this vital piece of information. Mr. Schmidt seemed to be taken aback, and he made a mental note about curries. My display of defiance was deliberate, to keep Mr. Schmidt quiet till I finished my dinner in peace.

I could sense something rather large coming my way, and was trying to delay the inevitable. When I was digging through my third round of dessert, which was hot *gulabjamun* with vanilla man with a demonic smile.

"You want to watch the movie in a theatre?" I overacted in disbelief.

"Yes, please, and not the movie halls in the mall but the Indian movie halls that you have everywhere. Mark said that is where you will have the experience of your lifetime."

Mark was lucky that he wasn't nearby. I would have definitely kicked him in the stomach, punched him in his face and would have quickly run over to the buffet to get some steamy hot *rasam* (spicy Indian soup) to pour on him. I never get such violent thoughts usually, except on such special occasions.

Mr. Schmidt had been clearly briefed, and there was no escape. I asked sarcastically, "Has Mark also told you which movie to watch?" I was getting really irritated with this unknown Mark guy.

Mr. Schmidt looked elated, didn't notice the sarcasm and said "Yes. The Robot. The Rajnikanth movie."

My vocabulary is quite inadequate to describe the exact feelings I had for the next five minutes. I wanted to become Rajnikanth Thalaivar myself, find and punish Mark and give a stern warning to Mr. Schmidt too. I was thinking which Thalaivar stunt would be best suited for this purpose but before I could zero down on it. Mr. Schmidt said, "We hear a lot about Rajnikanth and his movies."

"No chance, Mr. Schmidt," I brought up my widest and most artificial smile, reserved for such occasions, "Rajni movies are always houseful. You have to book tickets months in advance. Once Rajni himself wanted to buy a ticket for his own movie and even he could not get it." I cracked this P.J. a.k.a. poor joke and laughed loudly myself, another desperate attempt to somehow escape the situation.

Mr. Schmidt smiled lightly, indicating he noticed and liked the joke, but he was not ready to give up.

"But Latha said she can easily get it."

"Latha, who?"

"Latha Gopalkrishnan. Our account manager."

"What?" I shouted so loudly that the patrons at nearby tables paused in their conversation, and looked at us. Nobody was accustomed to see their fellow countrymen screaming at a white man. But I was feeling surrounded. This afternoon I had pretended to be very busy, and my team had taken Mr. Schmidt out for lunch. In an attempt to impress him, they must have given him all this unnecessary and potentially dangerous information.

"In fact, she is getting three tickets for us for the show tomorrow afternoon. She insisted that she wants to join us to watch the movie for the seventh time," Mr. Schmidt drove the last nail into the coffin.

I didn't know how to react. I had lost interest in the seventh round of dessert - hot *jalebi*, which I had specially ordered for myself. Despite eating so many sweet things I started getting a sour taste at the back of my tongue. If I had three bullets at that time, I would have fired first at Mark, second at Latha and third in the air to threaten Mr. Schmidt to drop the demand for the movie and give me my next order without any procrastination. For now, however, I had to deal with a 3 o'clock show the next day.

Latha (pronounced as Lataa) was the movie buff of our office, whom we had nicknamed the "talking Wikipedia of Indian movies." Nobody quite figured out how, but she knew everything about every movie. She would know the ratings of a movie even before it was released and would warn everyone to avoid bad movies, but she would watch them anyway. She always got tickets to good movies on the day of the release. She would also know all the behind the camera stories including shooting locations, budget, who was initially offered the role, why did he/she reject, how much they were paid, who had an affair with whom on the sets, everything! If she had put 10% of the energy she spent on movies on work, I wouldn't be dealing with Mr. Schmidt but his boss's boss.

I am a movie-averse guy, especially Indian movies. For me, watching a movie is like watching a match fixed cricket game. You know the end result, you just need to see who is doing what. I like songs but don't like to watch them in movies. It just prolongs the movie and is such a waste of time. I like to watch Hollywood movies that are crisp and focused. I couldn't have survived the ordeal of taking Mr. Schmidt to the movie all by myself. I was glad Mr. Schmidt had found Latha. I could sit back and relax, or probably sleep through the movie.

The next day, Manjunath dropped Mr. Schmidt and me at Urvashi theatre near Lal Bagh, amidst the cacophony of slow moving traffic. Latha was waiting for us. She was about 5 feet 5 inches tall, with a dark complexion, and a slim figure by Indian standards. Her jet-black hair ran well below her shoulders, and she had large, bright expressive eyes. She had chosen her most colorful and bright dress for this occasion. On the base of greenish-yellow there were innumerable shades of blue color and she had a contrast colored *dupatta* to make up for any unintended shortfall in colors. She was also wearing a *gajra* - a string of fragrant jasmine flowers - in her hair. Mr. Schmidt was dazed by this assault on his senses.

"This way, Sir." Latha pointed at a closed gate. As we moved closer, the security guard saluted us, acknowledged Latha and held the door open for us. Latha ushered us to a special room reserved for VIPs one level above the balcony floor. We sat down on a maroon colored leather sofa. The walls were decorated with posters of hit movies of past. One wall was dedicated to the photographs of all famous movie stars with the theatre owner. Latha was elated to see these photographs again but I wasn't interested. We were served typical south Indian filter coffee in steel cups, but Mr. Schmidt opted for a diet coke.

"We still have more than half an hour for the movie to start so I thought of arranging this place for us." said Latha in a Tamil accent. This served as a nice icebreaker.

Mr. Schmidt asked, "How long is this movie?"

"Just three hours" Latha replied enthusiastically. I knew where this was going. I explicitly exited the conversation by pretending to look at the photo wall.

Just as I thought, Mr. Schmidt fired his next salvo, "Why are Indian movies three hours long? Why don't they create movies of one and half hours like rest of the world does?"

I shook my head, but Latha was quite elated to hear this. She looked as if finally, she had found someone who could do justice to the treasure trove of knowledge she had gathered about Indian movies. She turned in her seat forty-five degrees to face Mr. Schmidt and started her explanation.

"Please get the facts right. India is the largest movie producer in the world. About one thousand movies are produced in India every year across various languages and regions. The second largest movie producer is Hollywood that produces five hundred movies. So India is the volume leader of movies. Leaders are supposed to create trends, not follow them."

"Wow. Mr. Schmidt had finally found his match," I said to myself.

"But still, why three hours? What is so great about three hours?" Mr. Schmidt was in no mood to give up.

"To understand this, we need to understand the history of Indian movies first," said Latha. Mr. Schmidt put his hand to his chin and reclined slightly forward, indicating very high interest in the history of Indian cinema. I was still near the wall but was all ears to hear what Latha was about to say.

"Cinema arrived in India in 1913 when Dadasaheb Phalke produced a silent movie called 'Raja Harischandra', based on a Sanskrit epic. The format of the movie was guided by the entertainment options that cinema replaced. The main competition for movies back then was musical dramas. This was a very unique entertainment option that ruled the sub-continent. The drama would usually be based on mythological stories and characters. The story was narrated through dialogues and songs both. Songs were an integral part of the story. These were based on classical ragas. The actors would not only act and say their dialogues but also sing during the play. What is most astonishing is, these dramas were a very advanced form of entertainment."

"Ancient dramas were an advanced form of entertainment? That is so incredible," Mr. Schmidt was at his sarcastic best but usually Indians get misled by words like "incredible," "unbelievable." They mistake the sarcasm for a compliment. Latha was no different, and she continued with even more enthusiasm.

"Yeah! Would you believe it? They were highly interactive, customizable, open-ended performances. If the audience liked a song, they would request the on-stage actor to sing it again. And again and again. The actors would take pride in how many 'once more' requests they got during any performance. A good play, which would be scripted for three hours, could take anywhere between four to six hours to come to an end. In fact, actors would consider it a disgrace if the drama ended in exactly three hours, without any 'once more' request."

"That is so amazing!" Mr. Schmidt was still unsure about where this was leading.

"Indian cinema was competing against this advanced, interactive form of entertainment. Naturally, some basic things such as songs could not be altered. In those days, a significant chunk of the audience used to travel from nearby towns and villages. So the entertainment duration had to be longer than their travel time. It is equally true these days as well. Various experiments with altering movie durations have failed."

"That sounds pretty logical." Did Mr. Schmidt back out? My experience during the last three days told me it could not be. Maybe he was thinking of another question. Latha gave some instructions to the guy standing at the door. The guy nodded and left.

"I asked him to see if there are any complimentary CDs of the movie songs available at the office. It would be a nice memento for Mr. Schmidt," Mr. Schmidt's face brightened up.

He found his next topic : "Why do Indian movies have so many songs?" Latha was quick to reply, "As I just said, there were quite a few things inherited from earlier forms of entertainment. Songs were one of them."

"But why would you continue with such a tradition?"

Latha was up for the challenge, "Firstly, songs have always been an integral part of the movies. The story wraps around the songs, it moves ahead through songs. Secondly, songs don't just stay on the silver screen. They are omnipresent on music channels, radio stations, and cultural programs. It's similar to song albums released in the West. A movie is a story and song album rolled into one. Lastly, songs are an integral part of the revenue streams of Indian movies. They generate about 10-12% of the total revenue for the movies. The song rights are sold even before the movie is produced. They are used as teasers for upcoming movies."

Latha had resolved this query like she would do for a consulting project, by systematically building an argument that addresses all the important facets of the core issue.

"What about the dance? What exactly is this Bollywood dance? How come everyone knows it? Do they teach that in school?"

Both Latha and I laughed loudly. Since Latha was handling Mr. Schmidt so well I didn't see any reason to hang around near the photo wall. I took my seat and started sipping the authentic south Indian filter coffee. Latha continued, "India has a great tradition in dancing. There are over hundred classical dance forms in India. All of them have their own rules, rhythms and moves."

."..and Bollywood dance is one of them, right?" Mr. Schmidt's impatience got the better of him.

"No, not at all," Latha sounded irritated. Knowing south Indian traditions, I reckoned that Latha would have learned Indian classical dance from the age of five. She would never allow a comparison between those dance forms and Bollywood.

"Actually, Bollywood dance is not a defined dance form at all. We just call it dance. This is an ever-evolving type of dance fueled by Indian movies. The choreographers use their creativity and come up with new dance moves for virtually every new song. In doing so, they borrow dance moves from every conceivable dance type."

"Does Bollywood dance also have rigid rules?"

"The only rule in this type of dance is that 'there is no rule'. You just catch the beat and express yourself. Any rhythm is fine as long as you catch it and go with it. On the same number, same rhythm, if you feel like dancing differently, go ahead!"

Mr. Schmidt laughed heartily. He looked at his watch and looked around. We still had ten minutes to kill. Mr. Schmidt noticed the poster of the movie 'Robot', with Rajnikanth posing with Aishwarya Rai. He pointed at that and asked, "Isn't that an obviously mismatched pair? Why are Indian heroines always beautiful and heroes get away with any kind of looks?"

This was the most offending question of the evening so far. Commenting about Rajnikanth's looks to a die-hard Rajni fan was no less than insulting the Indian flag. Latha paused for a moment and looked at the poster. I am sure she must have said a small prayer to request almighty Thalaivar Rajnikanth to forgive Mr. Schmidt.

Latha continued rather dryly. "Indian movies are designed as a perfect getaway for the average Indian. He leads a life, which is far from perfect. There are struggles, frustrations, unfulfilled dreams, and nothing goes as per his plan most of the times. Movies for average men and women in India are not just entertainment. It is a get away. They get really involved in movies."

"That's an interesting perspective!" It wasn't Mr. Schmidt.

It was me. I could totally relate to this.

"The man subconsciously relates to the protagonist. In those three hours he is transformed into the on-screen hero. So the hero has to look as close to him as possible. The average Indian knows he is not too handsome. So slightly above average looking heroes have done well in Indian movies. Once transformed, the hero has to get the most beautiful looking girl. This average Indian subconsciously romances the most beautiful girl, dances with her, sings for her. The heroine has to look beautiful, an average looking heroine is not okay. The average Indian already has an average looking girl. In movies he wants the best looking girl."

"What about the female audience? Why don't they demand the most handsome hero? Why do they settle for next-door looks?" Mr. Schmidt persisted.

"Women give more weightage to the overall character. They don't select their partners based on looks alone but based on mental connection. That's where heroes in Indian movies score well. Irrespective of looks the hero in Indian movies always connects with the heroine. He is the nicest person around and connects well with all female characters. Even if he is playing a criminal, he always wins the sympathy of the audience, predominantly the female audience. His looks therefore don't matter, mental connection does."

"Wow. That's an amazing explanation," Mr. Schmidt exclaimed.

"How do you know all this?" I was puzzled.

"Well I am a die-hard movie fan and I also read books like - Why men want sex and women need love. I thought of the explanation of looks of hero-heroines after I read the book."

"But now it's time to go and watch the Thalaivar in action... and... if I may, Mr. Schmidt, please don't ask me questions during the movie. I want to enjoy the movie fully."

Mr. Schmidt laughed out loud and said, "Ok."

"Why couldn't I think of such an easy solution to stop his barrage of questioning?" I thought to myself. Women have this incredible ability to find a simple solution to some daunting problems faced by men. They have the approach and attitude to deliver a difficult message in a simple way.

Watching 'Robot' in the movie theatre was an experience of a lifetime - not just for Mr. Schmidt but also for me. It was interactivity with entertainment media at its best. As soon as Chitti Robot came to life on screen, one section of the audience stood up and clapped in admiration. There were whistles, claps and slogan shouting. Some of the audience also showered coins on the screen during songs. Latha was right. Even after 100 years, the Indian audience hadn't really come out of a live entertainment mindset. They were acting as though Rajnikanth and Aishwarya were present on stage. Mr. Schmidt enjoyed this thoroughly for once. We were sitting in a private box, just the three of us. Mr. Schmidt got up and did his Bollywood dance mimicking the on screen actions. He borrowed some coins to throw on the screen. He clapped and whistled when others did. I don't know how much he understood the movie but he thoroughly enjoyed it. I thanked Latha profusely for being there with me.

Next day I went to see him off. He was waiting for me in the coffee shop. He welcomed me with the broadest smile in all of his four days, shook hands, and placed his left hand over my right. He was very thankful for letting him 'explore' India as per the guidelines provided by Mark.

"Let me introduce you to my friend, philosopher and guide - Mark," he pointed towards a man - who looked nothing like the 'Mark' of my imagination. If I had met him elsewhere, I would have mistaken him for an exceptionally fair Indian sage. He had a long flowing white beard, long hair tied in a ponytail, exceptional calmness on his face and steady eyes. I felt a little embarrassed that I had formed an adverse opinion about such a spiritual looking person without even seeing him. I was too confused to say anything.

"Yeah, this is the same Mark who guided me to explore India in a systematic manner. He has lived in India for the last 10 years. For the last 5 years he lives and works at Auroville in Pondicherry," Mr. Schmidt said.

I tried to say something but my jaw dropped further. Auroville in Pondicherry is a town meant for those who are in pursuit of finding their inner selves. It doesn't belong to any religion or nationality. In fact, Auroville is meant to be a universal town where men and women of all countries are able to live in peace and progressive harmony, above all creeds, all politics and all nationalities. The purpose of Auroville is to realize human unity as per its Wikipedia page. I was running the rat race so hard that I had not visited it although it was so close. Here I was face to face with a man who had travelled across half the planet and was planning to live there for the rest of his life. I was quite ashamed of my self for harboring wrong notions about this person for no particular reason.

Mark, in his husky, calm voice, said, "I came to India as a tourist and travelled in all directions, taking in all possible experiences for five years. After initial apprehension I tried everything. I lived on street food, tap water, walked on every street, petted stray dogs, learnt to ride bikes while zigzagging through traffic, and learnt the secret language of honks. I also watched a lot of movies. I have travelled a lot but I have never found any country where the audience interacts with the movie in this way. They live their life partially through these movies. I just fell in love with the spirit of this country. I went sightseeing in other countries, but India is different. If you try to find things to see, you may be disappointed. But if you decide to explore and experience it, it can change your life."

"Then one day my French girlfriend came to visit me, and we went to Auroville. I did a short course in meditation there and I found my calling. I experienced the ultimate calmness in my mind that I decided to stay there for the rest of my life. I am also asking this guy, Mr. Schmidt to leave the corporate rat race and join me," he finished with a wink.

For the last three years, I had been planning to visit Auroville but my role in the corporate rush prevented me from doing it. I knew why

Mr. Schmidt was keen on exploring India and he was damn right. I was really embarrassed, overwhelmed and introspective.

"Mark has convinced me to go with him to Pondicherry. I have got my ticket rescheduled and I am about to leave with Mark. I didn't tell you before because I wanted you to meet Mark. I have told him about the wonderful experiences I was able to have because of you and the explanations you and Latha gave me. Even Mark is impressed by the way you related Indian movies to the life of a common man. Thank you Mr. Vaidya for everything. I will see you soon."

Still, I couldn't say anything. I just shook hands with Mr. Schmidt and Mark, mentally apologized to him and appreciated him. I waved good-bye to both of them and left the hotel.

Mr. Schmidt gave us a lot of business before his company got sold off. He became a good friend and a die-hard Indian movie fan. I started watching Indian movies in the theatre yet again. I couldn't bring myself to dance with the crowd or shower coins on the screen but I no longer look down on those who do it. On Mr. Schmidt's insistence, I went to Pondicherry for a week to attend Mark's meditation workshop. It was a phenomenal experience. I am waiting for my calling to stop running the rat race.

Mr. Schmidt now travels to Pondicherry every year, and carries a lot of Indian movie CDs on his way back. When I met him last he said, "Mr. Vaidya, I understood why Indians are crazy about movies, after I became crazy about them myself."

4

WHY DO INDIANS LOVE CRICKET?

I looked at my watch nervously, fiddled with my pen and glanced outside the window from our office in Mont Kiara, an upmarket locality in Kuala Lumpur. Dark clouds had started to gather on the horizon.

A little while ago, when I had stepped out for lunch with my team, the sun was blazing. We were all dressed in our customary black business suits with brightly colored ties. As we had walked out of an air-conditioned office, we had realized that we were not dressed appropriately for the weather. "This is one British legacy that we still carry faithfully," Aadil, my Malaysian colleague had exclaimed, "I wonder why we still carry it forward?" He had a valid point. I had agreed as I had started to sweat under the collar and had to loosen the tie. I had removed my jacket, folded it and carried it on my left arm. "Some legacies are initiated by its perpetrators, but are wholeheartedly carried on by followers. So it is hard to determine whether the legacy should belong to the Perpetrators or followers," I had said. I had probably sounded completely incomprehensible, so nobody had said anything further.

I remembered this incident, while reclining in my chair in the conference room, and I smiled to myself. My colleague was presenting to the group and trying to build an argument to sell his ideas. I should have been listening to him but my mind was just not there. I was fidgety and inattentive.

By now, the black clouds had taken over the sky. I could see a green hill, which had started appearing greener under the light that filtered through the black clouds. It was flanked by a slew of high end, high-rise buildings making the hill appear shorter than it actually was. I could see a couple of cranes peeping from behind the farthest buildings indicating that the developers were not done yet.

I was thinking to myself, "I should expect the view to change again in the next 6 months. When I came here in 2006 for the first time, the entire space between our office and the hill was empty. Standing in the conference room and looking at the hill was a relaxing experience. But all the construction took away the view of the hill bit by bit."

My thoughts were getting more and more random. As I looked out, I knew that we were not far away from yet another thunderstorm. Kuala Lumpur receives the world's highest number of thunderstorms in a year. "Why should that happen?" I wondered, "People in this country are so peace-loving and cheerful. Why should they be struck with so many thunderstorms?" I didn't know why I was not able to focus on the meeting.

A distant voice in my head was telling me that I was missing something important. I had checked all my official appointments, and I knew that I hadn't missed anything. It was not my wife's birthday. I had checked three times if it was our anniversary but it wasn't. But the voice in my head wouldn't go away. I realized that this was not the proper way to attend the meeting. At the next logical pause in the presentation, I called out, "Guys, have you noticed this?" and pointed to the skies. Air-conditioned buildings cut you off from the elements. Ironically, Google is the only way to know the weather outside. My intervention had a desired impact. My team decided to call it a day as the local colleagues wanted to rush home before it started to rain.

Usually, the traffic in Kuala Lumpur is very bad in the evenings, and rain makes it worse. Travel time of thirty to forty minutes can shoot up to two to three hours because of rains. My colleagues rushed out. We allocated the work to be completed at home and decided to reconvene the next morning at 9 am. Soon I was all alone in the conference room, still wondering what I had missed.

Another fifteen-twenty minutes might have passed, when my mental quest for the answer was interrupted by a knock on the door. Vikram, Mohan and Satish rushed in. Dressed in the usual long-sleeved light colored formal shirts and dark colored formal trousers, their body language, facial expressions and enthusiasm told me they had something exciting to share.

All three of them were bright MBAs who had joined us 3-4 years ago. They had moved from India to Malaysia after campus recruitments. They used to stay close to our office and they had explored all the fun places nearby. "Boss, India Vs Pakistan. World-cup Semi-finals starting anytime. Do you want to join us?" they said. There was a flash of lightning, not in the skies but in my mind. This was what I was missing! I had completely forgotten about the epic battle between my home country and arch-rivals on the cricket field.

How could I miss that for goodness sake? Adrenaline and all the other related hormones surged through my veins, I shut my laptop, put it in the bag in one smooth action, sprang to my feet and with a beaming smile on the face said, "Let's go!" We dashed to the lift lobby and pressed the elevator button multiple times to make sure it is pressed, secretly and insanely hoping that our actions would accelerate the elevator.

"Where are we going?" I asked them with the excitement and curiosity of a child.

"Our den," they said with a wink.

They led me through the by-lanes near our office. The footpaths were lined with eateries and cafes. As the sun set, these places came alive, buzzing with activity. Most of the cafes would arrange for seating on the sidewalks, which gave a cool, relaxed feel. Their usual patrons had not arrived yet, so most of the cafes and eateries were empty but getting ready for business. It was about to rain so they were not sure whether they should arrange for the seating or wait for the thunder storm to pass by. Soon we arrived at an Irish pub, which was buzzing with activity.

"Here we are!" they chorused as we stormed inside.

This Irish pub had an old rusty look. The olive green exteriors had faded beyond recognition and the interiors were long overdue for renovation. At some point in time this pub must have been quite swanky, which you could tell from the layout and choice of furniture. Most of the seating was high tables with bar stools with tables of varying seating capacities to cater to different group sizes. The wooden bar display looked really old, underlying wooden facade was visible as the deep brown color had chipped at various places. Sometime in the past, the bar would have been adorned with decorative, expensive liquor bottles but it was now a shadow of its glorious past. A few familiar bottles were kept at an approachable height but the rest of the facade was empty. I was sure it would be taking a lot of mental preparation for the bartenders and waiters to get inside their worn out uniform every day. A few noisy air-conditioners on the walls were getting ready to keep this place cool and I was wondering why my colleagues had brought me to this worn out place, so proudly.

Everyone in that place seemed to know my colleagues. They waved and smiled at the staff. One of the waiters removed a reserved placard from a table for us and rushed inside to get the menu. I was still not sure what was happening when Satish probably sensing my uneasiness tapped my shoulder and pointed to a screen above the main entrance. It was a LCD projector with a large screen to show a live telecast of the cricket match and we were proudly occupying the front seat. I was proud of my team and my decision to recruit them.

The pub owner must have been a wise man. He had come up with this ingenious idea of attracting sports crazy fans by showing niche sports matches that are not easily available elsewhere in the city. I noticed that he had rearranged his seating arrangement to create a dividing line in the middle of his pub. He had placed flags of two competing countries on either sides of the screen, subtly indicating which side the fans were expected to be seated. The LCD projector was hung from the ceiling and speakers were attached to the wall to maximize the floor space. They didn't need to hang any banner or create a special World Cup menu. Cricket fans were pouring in, dressed in team uniforms, carrying flags and some of them even had face paint.

The game was about to start as the two captains walked out for the toss.

> *Toss, 1400hrs : Dhoni tosses. Afridi calls heads. It's tails. India will bat! "We need runs on the board in this tense game," says Dhoni. Is this the biggest game of your life?, Shastri asks Dhoni, who says it's difficult to say because he can't remember how he felt before previous crunch games.*

There was a huge round of applause peppered with whistles and shouts. The ambience was electric and all of us were set for a thrilling match ahead. At each table the discussions were about who should open the innings, what should the batting order be.

I was looking around as my colleagues were discussing the winning score. I spotted a man, perhaps on the other side of his 50, dressed in a loose green half shirt and cargo trousers, with a well grown white beard, tanned white skin, slim and average height. He didn't look like a cricket fan. He looked more like a regular patron who visited for a daily dose of beer among friendly people. He obviously looked surprised to see his favorite joint overcrowded with so many unknown people. The pub staff was running around fulfilling orders and the patrons were worried about getting a view of the screen rather than finding a place to sit. Nobody paid any attention to him. It must have started raining outside as he decided to hang around, although he was struggling to find a place to sit.

There came my 'Murari-Lal' moment. The Murari- lal moment is a concept in a 1971 Hindi movie Anand. The protagonist played by Rajesh Khanna has his days numbered due to stomach cancer. He wants to spend them happily and meet as many people as possible. So he takes off to meet unknown people walking on the streets, calls them Murari-lal and starts talking to them. He argues that there are waves coming out of people and when we catch them we start liking that person for no apparent reason.

When I looked at the stranger again, I decided to act on my Murari-lal instinct by waving at him. He was quite surprised and unsure. We were occupying a prime table for six among four of us. I waved again and pointed to the empty seat on my right and called him over. He gladly accepted the invitation and walked over to our table.

"Hi, my name is Vivek," I introduced myself. The fellow was soft spoken. He introduced himself but his introduction coincided with Sehwag and Sachin walking out to the middle of the field. There was a huge roar. I couldn't hear his name. I think he said his name was John but I could not be sure. I decided that his name was John anyway. John was grateful that he got a good seat and he started to look around to understand what was really happening. My hunch that he was a regular patron turned out to be true as one of the waiters brought him a pitcher of beer and some nuts without being asked.

14 : 29 The hype and the build-up is over. Sehwag on strike, Tendulkar at the non-strikers.

Umar Gul with the new ball, ready to run in from over the wicket. This moment cannot have come soon enough.

Gul's leaping and stretching at the start of his run up. He looks pumped ... Let's play, says the umpire.

0.3. Umar Gul to Sehwag, FOUR, driven through covers for four. The ball was a touch too full outside off, Sehwag says so still and brings his bat down swiftly to crash the ball through the infield

I heard the loudest roar ever. All Indian supporters sprang to their feet. They were hysterical. I must say that it was the most thrilling way to watch a cricket match! A room full of cricket fans, with a huge screen, your own group to discuss your thoughts and a free flow of drinks and food, what else could one ask for?

I remembered, in my childhood, watching a full day cricket match used to be a family affair. My siblings, cousins, father, uncles and even my grandfather would occupy their vantage seats in front of a black and white TV with lots of tit-bits to munch on. Every run would be cheered for, every missed chance would be booed and we used to get very emotional if we were losing the match. All the neighboring houses would have similar settings, we could hear loud roars from our neighbors when a wicket fell or an exciting shot was played. All those memories came flooding back to me as I got myself ready to watch this epic battle, far away from home yet very close in memories.

John was trying to ask me if that was cricket. I didn't have time to answer such a naïve question. I had come there to enjoy, not to educate a stranger about the sports I felt passionately for. John realized this. He took out his iPad and started browsing it.

He seemed comfortable amidst chaos.

2.1 : Umar Gul to Sehwag, FOUR, a half-volley on his leg stump dismissed by Sehwag with a crisp flick off his pads. He hit that in the air but there was no fielder anywhere near midwicket.

2.2 : Umar Gul to Sehwag, FOUR, too straight again, not as full, but Sehwag stays in his crease and whips the ball off his pads through midwicket. Still no fielder there.

2.3 : Umar Gul to Sehwag, no run, short of a length around the hips, Sehwag tucks the ball off his body towards the man at square leg.

2.4 : Umar Gul to Sehwag, FOUR, too straight again and Sehwag flicks, this time past the fielder at square leg and the ball races across this fast outfield towards the boundary before the fielder at long leg can get to it.

2.5 : Umar Gul to Sehwag, FOUR, that's the fourth of the over. A slower ball outside off stump. The length was

*short and there was width. Sehwag waited for it and cut
the ball hard through point.*

*2.6 : Umar Gul to Sehwag, (no ball) FOUR, the fifth!
And it's a front-foot no-ball as well. Too full outside off
and Sehwag drills the ball off the front foot through extra
cover. Gul is rattled. Sehwag on the charge.*

India 27/0 V Sehwag 25* (14b 6x4)

Ravi Shastri - the commentator - was searching for appropriate
words to describe the proceedings but in that pub in Mont Kiara nobody
needed any words. The decibel level substituted the need for any words.
Claps, whistles or any other means of producing a loud sound wasn't
enough. So some groups started banging on the tables and mimicked
playing the drums on them. Whichever object made a loud sound was
useful. To describe it as a cacophony was an understatement. Perhaps,
the atmosphere there could not do justice to the excitement levels. I
now realized why newer pubs wouldn't screen cricket matches. From
the corner of my eyes, I noticed John had one of his hands on his ear
and a smile on his face as he was googling about cricket on his iPad.

I have always wondered why loud sounds do not impact those
creating it, why quiet people feel like shutting their ears. Solutions to
some problems can be so counter- intuitive. Next time you are stuck
in a cacophony rather than closing your ears, shout loudly. That might
work better.

*3.6 : Abdul Razzaqto Tendulkar, FOUR, pure timing
and placement. Tendulkar moves forward and drives with
Zen-like calm through extra cover. Mid-off should have
dived to try and cut it off but he didn't*

India 39/0 SR Tendulkar 8* (8b 1x4)

This was a sensational start to the Indian innings. This is what I had come here for. It was an exhilarating experience. I had always wondered why I felt so excited while watching a cricket match. What is so great about a leather ball traveling at 140 kilometer per hour hitting a piece of wood and disappearing equally fast into the crowds? Why does this sight create such an excitement in people like me? Why do I feel that connection with the cricketers? Why do I feel like I know them?

> *Wahab Riaz to Sehwag, OUT, Taufel has given Sehwag out and he's asked for a review against the lbw decision immediately. He didn't even check with Tendulkar. Brilliant decision from Taufel. That ball pitched just in line with the leg stump, short of a length, and skidded on to Sehwag, beating the batsman's attempted flick off the back foot. That ball didn't bounce as much as Sehwag thought it would. He was on his toes playing the shot. The only doubt was whether it pitched in line, it did. Pakistanis are ecstatic.*

> *V Sehwag lbw b Wahab Riaz 38 (32m 25b 9x4 0x6) SR: 152.00*

> *India 48/1 V Sehwag 38 (25b 9x4)*

With Sehwag's departure our initial excitement waned and as our voices became hoarse and legs got tired, adrenaline in the blood was in short supply so it was time to order the next pitcher.

I looked at my colleagues with a smile and raised my glass to say 'thank you'. They raised it back which meant 'anytime'. We now had some bandwidth available to see what John was up to.

I gave a warm friendly smile to John, to break the ice. He smiled back. It was a mature, controlled yet transparent smile. He had a mystic air around him. In several years of my observation, I have found that some people have a very transparent face. It does not hide what is on their minds. John was certainly one of them.

"So cricket is followed like a religion in India. I can sense it here," John said. By now, the decibel levels had come back to normal, the loudest person being Ravi Shastri the commentator, so normal conversation was possible.

"Well yes. We grew up watching this game and frankly this is the only game Indians are good at. So it is fun to watch our team doing well," I replied. He was looking straight into my eyes and had very positive body language - his face told me he wanted to hear more. So I started narrating the story of my association with cricket.

"Cricket and English are the legacies left behind by the British colonial rule. But now India is the new home of cricket," as I said this, I remembered my incomprehensible remark about legacy which belongs more to the followers than the perpetrators that I had made in the morning. I realized that I had been thinking about cricket subconsciously, since morning and the profound statement was its mystic manifestation. John must have read this in some article just now, so he nodded in agreement.

By now my three colleagues also wanted to join the guest. Mohan had joined us but he was not a die-hard fan like all the others. In fact he was the skeptic in the team. He could find fault with anything and everything around. Why should cricket be any exception?

"Cricket is not even the national sport of India. It was no doubt a very popular game but it didn't have the status of a religion till thirty years ago," he said.

"Was it the world cup victory in 1983?" asked John as he ran his hands through his white beard. We were surprised and impressed at the same time. Not just with John, by whom I was getting intrigued, but also with Google. Give a reasonably intelligent man a good Internet connection and Google, and within an hour he will sound like an expert.

"Yes! That's right," I did not want to hide my appreciation as I set foot in a time machine mentally, going back to the 1983 World Cup finals between India and the West Indies. "I was about 12 years old then but it almost seems like yesterday. I had to stay up late in the night to watch the match. It was so thrilling to watch our team fight against the mighty West Indies. They were the best team in the world back then. I never thought that we would win it till it happened."

John nodded in appreciation and asked, "And how strong was Indian team back then?" He was really good at developing the conversation.

"Oh! Back then Indian team was the biggest underdog. Led by a twenty four year old captain, it was a bunch of talented but rooky players. Nobody gave them a chance. They fought tooth and nail through out to win the Cup and bring home the glory."

John pulled a notepad out of his bag and took out his pen and scribbled something on a piece of paper. What was he doing I could not help but wonder!

7.5 : Wahab Riaz to Tendulkar, FOUR, too full with width outside off, Tendulkar moves towards the ball, crouches on one knee and plays the perfect square drive through point

7.6 : Wahab Riaz to Tendulkar, no run, short of a length closer to off stump, Tendulkar moves towards the off, gets behind the line and plays towards cover

India 65/1 SR Tendulkar 23* (21b 4x4)

There was a loud roar as Sachin hit a breathtaking shot, the ball travelled just ahead of the fielder to keep him interested but still crossed the rope. This was a familiar sight when Tendulkar was batting which caused excitement among the subdued fan- folks.

I glanced around in that relatively dim warm light, the pub was jam-packed and fans were still pouring in. The rain had probably stopped. A few Pakistani fans were still holding on but the Indian fans were clearly the largest group. A few white men, probably from other cricket playing nations, were enjoying this match too. The segregated seating arrangement for fans of respective countries had broken down. In fact, there were a lot of people standing at the farthest end, with their drinks to watch the match, without any hope of getting a seat. Getting a good view of the screen was far more important than getting a seat. Thanks to my colleagues, we had the best of both worlds.

"Do you play cricket?" John asked me.

I was slightly surprised by this question. "Almost every Indian plays cricket. That's the game we have grown up with. That is our first touch point for any sports," I was going on and on with sentences that essentially communicated the same viewpoint.

"But how? It requires such a large playground, so much equipment, eleven players in a team. Is that easily available everywhere?" John had a specific query.

I knew where he was coming from. I smiled and said, "Oh.. no, no. I have never played cricket on such a big ground with this kind of equipment. We play cricket wherever we get space and with whatever equipment we can find."

I could see a combination of question mark and exclamation mark on John's face. But I was telling the truth. It's like kids in football playing nations playing their football anywhere.

"We play on small grounds, by-lanes, corridors, even slightly large rooms. Wherever we can find a place. We adapt the game to the available place and number of players. It is quite flexible so everyone can play."

John was intrigued. He scribbled something more on his paper.

John's curiosity was growing, "As I am watching this game, I realize that the players have very different physical traits. What physical trait is best suited to play cricket? Are tall players better than shorter ones? Or slim players better than the fatter ones?"

I smiled as I remembered various sizes and shapes of cricket players with the likes of Joel Garner and Courtney Walsh (height above 2 meters) on one side and Parthiv Patel and Vishwanath (both 1.6 meters) on the other side. Merv Hughes, David Boon (both overweight cricketers) on one side and Azharuddin and Srinath (both lanky, underweight cricketers) on the other. This was an easy question.

"None at all. You can be tall or short, fat or lean, young or old, broad or lanky. Cricket gives you an equal chance. Sachin is just five feet five inches but he is able to dominate a bowler over six feet. Arjuna Ranatunga, the captain of Sri Lanka's world cup winning team, was an obese person. Mohammad Azharuddin who holds the world record for scoring three centuries in his first three matches was a lanky, underweight sportsman."

I was struggling to find more examples when Vikram butted in. Vikram was a man of few words but when he spoke he would bring up the most relevant point.

He said, "The bowler who holds the record for maximum wickets, Muralidharan from Sri Lanka, has double jointed wrists which in many countries is considered a handicap. I don't know of any other game which provides a physically handicapped person an opportunity to play at an international level to create world records."

John was astonished. He again started scribbling something on his paper.

I gave an appreciative look to Vikram. Vikram was a born analyst. He was a structured thinker and would always talk as if he was making a final presentation to a client. We used to joke that even when he proposed to a girl he would do so with a SWOT analysis.

21.2 :Shahid Afridi to Tendulkar, FOUR, Top shot! Fifty up. Afridi tries to lure Tendulkar into another catch at cover. He flighted it up, slowed it down and tossed it outside off. Tendulkar stretched forward and hit this one over extra cover.

Every Indian fan in the pub got onto his feet and gave a standing ovation to the little master. Everyone knew that they wouldn't see Sachin batting again in the next World Cup and they would miss him very much. Everyone wanted to enjoy the moment and pay their respects to their favorite cricketer.

John noticed this. He had probably also read about Sachin.

"Why do Indians love Sachin Tendulkar so much?" he asked the inevitable question.

21.6 : Shahid Afridi to Tendulkar, FOUR, What a shot! It was full and just outside off. NO way that looked like it can be cut. Tendulkar pressed back, crouched, opened the bat-face and played the late cut. He steered it through vacant slips.

India 130/2 SR Tendulkar 56* (70b 9x4)

"That's why," all four of us said in chorus, pointing at the screen. We all laughed. "Great men think alike!" boasted Satish. "Or fools never differ," Mohan's skepticism continued. We all laughed again.

John's question about Sachin was a low full toss for Satish who was itching to hit it out of the park. He was a die-hard Sachin fan. Satish said, "Sachin is the best batsman in the modern era.

He is the highest run scorer and has scored the maximum number of hundreds."

"I read that," John interrupted Vikram to fine tune his question further, "I read about his records but is that the only reason Indians love him? I sense a kind of emotional connection with Sachin."

Satish knew what he was saying. He in turn fine-tuned his answer further, "Yes indeed! We feel for him. We saw him making his debut as a teenager. A baby faced, curly haired boy playing against veterans in Pakistan was an unbelievable sight. Can he really play well against these fast bowlers? We had wondered. If he did it, it would be a dream come true for 1 billion people in India."

Satish' passion about Sachin fueled his articulation. All of us were pulled in to his narration.

"I still remember it was a friendly match against Pakistan and Sachin hit a couple of sixes against a young leg spinner - Mushtaq Mohammad. Veteran leg spinner Abdul Qadir, walked up to Sachin and said, "Miyan, thoda hamein bhi maar ke dikhao." (Let me see if you can do the same if you play against me) It was a David Vs Goliath contest. Debutant Sachin - age sixteen Vs Abdul Qadir - age forty and one of the all-time great bowlers. Sachin wasn't even born when Abdul

Qadir had started playing cricket. We had never seen anything like it. We held our breath. In the next over, Sachin had hit 3 sixes and 2 fours. Abdul Qadir was dumbfounded. So were we." It was indeed a nice trip down the memory lane.

Satish wasn't done yet.

"A few days later, in a test match, Sachin was facing Waqar Younus - the fast bowler. One fast bouncer hit him on the nose and Sachin started bleeding profusely. We thought we were going to see this boy leave the field on a stretcher. But he wiped his blood and said - Mai khelega (I will play). The very next ball, he hit a straight drive for four. He had scored a moral victory against the archrivals. These scenes are firmly etched in our minds," Satish was at his eloquent best.

25.2 : Wahab Riaz to Kohli, OUT, Pakistan have taken a catch! Wahab strikes again! Caught at backward point. It landed on a length around off and angled away, Virat played a strange shot as if he was surprised by how it seamed away - Wahab hardly gets the ball to bend in - and had a weak waft at it. He just stabbed at it. Edge and pouched!

V Kohli c Umar Akmal b Wahab Riaz 9 (20m 21b 0x4 0x6) SR: 42.85

India 141/3 V Kohli 9 (21b)

Wahab Riaz to Yuvraj Singh, OUT, Crashing full swinging delivery! Sensational moment! Wahab, who was playing in this game instead of Shoaib, has done the job. What a little big moment. Pakistan huddle is on. It was full, it was pacy and it swung in beautifully past the hurried stab and crashed into the stumps. Clatter! It didn't land at all. He just took the pitch out of the equation

Yuvraj Singh b Wahab Riaz 0 (1m 1b 0x4 0x6) SR: 0.00

India 141/4 Yuvraj Singh 0 (1b)

Pakistan had their tails up. Dhoni edged a ball unconvincingly to beat third man to get a four Suddenly the game started looking shaky for Indians. But Sachin was still out there in the middle, so our hopes remained intact.

"As long as Sachin is playing, the Indian team has nothing to worry," said Satish. We all nodded.

John looked puzzled. "What do you mean by that?" he asked. Satish was not just an ordinary fan but also an ardent devotee of Sachin.

"Because he has won several matches for India singlehandedly."

"What do you mean singlehandedly?" asked John. "All by himself," said Satish.

"err...ummm" John didn't know what to ask next.

Vikram, the analyst, spotted the confusion. John could not understand how one payer can dominate the entire opposition team.

Vikram volunteered to explain, "What he means is, in many matches when everyone in the Indian team failed to score, only Sachin Tendulkar's batting helped India win the match."

"Really?" John's disbelief, confusion and curiosity rolled into a single word.

"Yeah!" Mohan and Satish joined in chorus.

"Well how is that possible?" John was still not convinced,

"Can one man defeat the entire team?"

"If a player is talented or in a very good form then it can happen," I tried to sound moderate to make the claim believable.

John took a pause to absorb this and said, "So you mean to say that Sachin Tendulkar is considered the God because he has won matches singlehandedly for India?"

Sachin and Dhoni went about building the innings steadily. There were no flashy shots, no aggression, just intelligent and sensible cricket.

Satish continued, "There is no doubt that Sachin is talented. But what sets him apart is his attitude to handle downturn and his humility. He was diagnosed with tennis elbow and for a few months he could not even hold a cricket bat. But he came back from the surgery, practiced and reached the peak of his career."

Mohan cleared his throat, Satish paused and we all looked at Mohan. He said, "To be famous in India you need to win the sympathy of masses. It happened to Amitabh Bachchan, when he got injured in fight scene while shooting for a movie. Why would Sachin be left behind?"

We wondered if there was anything that could escape Mohan's sarcasm. Satish was Mohan's schoolmate. He knew how to deal with it.

He ignored Mohan and continued, "Despite being on the top, Sachin is extremely humble. He always talks about his teammates and opponents with great respect. He never boasts about his achievements and stays humble. Even opponents and rivals have only praises for him."

36.6 : Saeed Ajmal to Tendulkar, OUT, finally, they've held one! Sachin falls. And guess who's there to take the catch? Afridi drops to his left to hold onto a stinging drive at short extra cover. 'If you want the job done right, then do it yourself,' he's thinking. Possibly. Relief flows visibly over the Pakistanis as they gather at the fall of the wicket. Plenty of smiles out there now.

*SR Tendulkar c Shahid Afridi b Saeed Ajmal 85 (160m
115b 11x4 0x6) SR: 73.91*

India 187/5 SR Tendulkar 85 (115b 11x4)

There were sighs and voices filled with disappointment in the Indian camp, overridden by jubilation, high-fives and whistles from the handful of Pakistani fans.

After a few minutes, there was a pin-drop silence in the Indian camp. John looked around, trying to control his smile. Every Indian fan was watching the sight in despair, with hands on their foreheads, with faces hidden in their palms. They banged the table in disappointment. Some packed up to go home. John was amused. He must be thinking that these Indian fans are crazy. How can they be so emotional when one player is out, that too after playing a good innings?

In order to explain this absurd situation I had to explain the real connection of Indians with Sachin.

"From my perspective," I went on to explain, "Sachin's status goes far beyond cricket. Sachin Tendulkar hails from a middle class family. He chased his dream against all odds, achieved it without any Godfather's help. He is brave, skillful, and perseverant. He has dominated the world unarguably for two decades, earned respect and limelight globally and yet stayed humble, rooted and a proud Indian. This is exactly what a common man in India wants to achieve. Sachin's emotional connection with one billion Indians comes from there. It is not just about cricket. It is about believing in yourself, fighting against all odds and succeeding, unarguably. Be it a player, be it a student, be it a corporate executive like me or be it that poor man on the street who has set out to earn something to make both ends meet, Sachin is a role model. Sachin is a dream in motion. Sachin is not just about cricket. He is about success in life."

My summary sounded more profound than I had expected. My team was visibly impressed. I felt good about myself. We forgot about Sachin's departure and signaled another drink for all of us including John. He was an integral part of our group now.

Suddenly there was another roar as Dhoni departed.

> *Wahab Riaz to Dhoni, OUT, well, that's one way to take the faulty catching out of the equation! Dhoni is rapped on the pad as he shuffles to off, huge appeal and Taufel has given him out! Dhoni wants a review though ... but it's not going to help, three reds as it pitches and hits him in line, definitely hitting the stumps and that's gone. India's hopes of making a defendable total are beginning to evaporate here*

> *MS Dhoni lbw b Wahab Riaz 25 (64m 42b 2x4 0x6) SR: 59.52*

> *India 205/6 MS Dhoni 25 (42b 2x4)*

We shifted our attention from John to the match on hand as we had started to feel tense. Suresh Raina, the young Turk, was left to salvage the situation with tail-enders. We were vociferously discussing what Raina should be doing.

Satish said, "Zaheer Khan tends to get a rush of blood and hits false shots. Raina should keep as much strike as he can and protect him from the fast bowlers." We all agreed.

John listened to us intently and asked why a certain batsman needed to be protected by the other.

He asked, "Is he not a batsman? He seems to be equipped with the same gear and seems to have it under control. Why is the other batsman required to take a lead or keep him away from the bowlers?"

Satish replied. "Well he is out there to bat but he is not really good at batting. He is primarily a bowler but rules of cricket need him to bat even though he is not good at it."

John was absolutely amazed. He looked at others and me with raised eyebrows to check if what he had just heard was true. We nodded in agreement. It was an interesting conversation with someone who was intelligent and interested in cricket and was questioning basics, which we never had.

He said, "This is quite unique right? I don't remember any other game where a player is forced to demonstrate the secondary skills. It is like asking the goalkeeper or defendant to lead the charge and score goal."

We were a bit surprised to hear this perspective. We had never looked at it that way but he was right. This was not a common practice in any other game. Satish said, "Yes, that's true. But these tail-enders treat this as an opportunity to shine. They take it as a challenge and try to surpass the expectations that are already quite low."

> *47.5 :Wahab Riaz to Khan, FOUR, this is comedic stuff! How has he hit that for four? Riaz fires one in full and fast, and it's a case of ball hitting bat, a leading edge loops over the infield and rolls to the wide third man boundary. Well, they're runs no matter how you get them*

Zaheer Khan hit a four as Satish was completing his sentence. He was pleased as the proof of his statement arrived right on time.

John smiled and said, "To me, the batsman appears to be the most important person. He takes his time to walk slowly to the pitch. The fielders, bowlers, umpires and spectators wait in anticipation. Then he takes his time to look around before he takes the strike. And he is allowed to do that before every ball is bowled."

This was a completely different perspective, which we had never heard before. Now we were intrigued. He Said, "I can imagine that walking in the middle with the entire batting gear with everyone waiting must be a pretty flattering experience especially for those who know they can't bat."

We were impressed. We had never thought about it that way. Was my theory about John being a psychic true? We nodded in agreement. Freshly ordered drinks had arrived. We raised our glasses and said, "Cheers to a new cricket fan!!!" We all laughed and got busy with our drinks.

Soon the Indian inning ended. Young Raina had done well and hit some meaty shots, bringing up a respectable total on board. It was a defendable total if the captain did all the right things.

India 260/9 in 50 overs. Well, fairly manic stuff out there at the end but India will be fairly happy to have reached 260 after losing their way a touch in the middle overs. Tendulkar will have to wait for that 100th ton, but top- scored with 85.

But hearing this from Vikram was a different experience altogether. Vikram presented his observation, "Captain Dhoni has a unique style of captaincy. He has opted for young budding players against more established players. He has respected senior players and has got their support and buy-in to his captaincy and then cracked down on the fence sitters. He brought in truckloads of young talent and built bench strength. Backed his players in difficult situations and motivated them to perform. He plays his favorites but it seems to work. He also has several strengths.

One : He appears very calm in any adverse situation.

Two : Leads from the front.

Three : Backs young players

Four : Regularly surprises opponent teams with his unusual moves and makes them work

Five : Has luck on his side at crucial junctures."

Vikram was on a roll. It was as if he was making a presentation to the client. "Now let's look at his and the team's weakness

One : The total on board is good but not great

Two : He does not have great bowlers who can rip through the opposition line up.

Three : Fielding could vary from good to mediocre to very bad

Four : Pakistan can play spinners well"

Vikram could have gone on and on but for a suppressed chuckling sound by John. All four for us were extremely surprised, slightly pissed and largely curious. John had become a bit too friendly.

John said, "You guys talk a lot about cricket." He was still trying to control his laughter. Pointing at me he said, "This guy has not really played cricket on such a playground. Has anyone else played at such a level or even at such a playground?"

All three of them looked down before Mohan started laughing and said, "This guy Vikram, who has analyzed the game so much, has never held a bat or ball in his hands."

Vikram was momentarily embarrassed and we all joined in the laughter. I patted Vikram's back implying it was okay. Vikram actually went aggressive and said, "I don't think you need to play cricket to determine the strategy. Even at our job, we recommend strategies to clients without actually running their operations."

He had a point. But John's point was something else. He said, "I agree. I have seen people enjoying other games, they dance, clap, get excited. But they don't analyze the game so much and talk about it so intensely."

I could not be sure but it sounded right. Meanwhile, Pakistan's innings had started.

0.1 : Khan to Kamran Akmal, FOUR, Cracking start from Kamran. He loves to square drive. He leaned forward to a length delivery angling away from him and drove it through cover point

The match was interestingly poised and we were all absorbed in watching it. "I had come here to watch the match not to educate a foreigner about cricket and answer all his silly questions," I thought to myself. My team caught the cues in my body language so they also focused on the screen and we started cheering the bowlers.

8.6 : Khan to Kamran Akmal, OUT, Done in by the slower one. And also done by his own favorite square drive. It was full and outside off stump, Kamran couldn't resist the temptation and reached out for his square drive. But he ended up slicing it straight to point.

Kamran Akmal c Yuvraj Singh b Khan 19 (40m 21b 3x4 0x6) SR: 90.47

Pakistan 44/1 Mohammad Hafeez 25* (33b 4x4) Z Khan 3-0-17-1

Indian fans went berserk. The decibel level went up again. We had to shout in each other's ears to communicate. All this meant, John was left completely ignored all of a sudden. He was welcome to join us in cheering and shouting but now we did not have time and patience for serious analytical stuff.

15.3 :Patel to Mohammad Hafeez, OUT, What was Hafeez thinking? Again, yet again, a lovely 30 -40 and he has combusted. He went for a paddle sweep, yeah a paddle sweep, to a full delivery outside off stump and edged it to Dhoni. Oh dear. Pressure? or over confidence?

Mohammad Hafeez c †Dhoni b Patel 43 (66m 59b 7x4 0x6) SR: 72.88

Pakistan 70/2 Asad Shafiq 8* (13b 1x4) MM Patel 5.3-1-24-1

After this, I got completely absorbed in the match. I didn't really notice where John was or what he was doing. We wanted to absorb the spirit of the match. We all danced, cheered, waved flags. All Indian fans in that pub became a single team. John was a smart man. He realized he could not hold conversation with us anymore, nor was he interested enough to watch the match. He got busy with his iPad again.

23.5 : Yuvraj Singh to Asad Shafiq, OUT, whoops! Shafiq's gone. Too straight and a touch too full to cut, Shafiq went back and tried to, he missed and the ball skidded straight past him and hit middle stump, the Indians get into a huddle. He was cramped for room and short of time to play that shot

Asad Shafiq b Yuvraj Singh 30 (61m 39b 2x4 0x6)

SR: 76.92

Pakistan 103/3 Younis Khan 11* (24b) Yuvraj Singh 2.5-0-9-1

25.4 : Yuvraj Singh to Younis Khan, OUT, caught at cover! A slow ball on a good length outside off, inviting Younis forward and into the drive. He takes the bait and spoons the ball towards Raina who leaps and takes the catch at head height. India are back in this ...

Younis Khan c Raina b Yuvraj Singh 13 (44m 32b 0x4 0x6) SR: 40.62

Pakistan 106/4 Misbah-ul-Haq 1* (3b) Yuvraj Singh 3.4-0-9-2

These were great fun moments spent with a group of strangers. You didn't need to know the other guy to give him a hi-five or a hug when the wicket fell. If someone started shouting slogans, the others would join in. If someone clapped others whistled in tandem. If your refill was delayed, a stranger on the next table was bound to pour beer from his pitcher. All boundaries within the groups had melted. Seating arrangements had collapsed. The spectator team was on a high with intoxicating cocktail of alcohol, cricket and camaraderie.

Umar Akmal and Misbah were doing a recovery act. Match was swinging decisively in favor of Pak when Dhoni makes an inspired balling change.

33.1 : Harbhajan Singh to Umar Akmal, OUT, bowled 'im! Bhajji strikes straight away, it wasn't the doosra - more of an arm ball - but Umar played it horribly, neither forward nor back and swishing hopefully through the line of the ball. It nipped past the bat and clattered into the off stump

Umar Akmal b Harbhajan Singh 29 (35m 24b 1x4 2x6) SR: 120.83

Pakistan 142/5 Misbah-ul-Haq 8* (24b) Harbhajan Singh 7.1-0-31-1

Cacophony transcended to the next octave. Suddenly, some Indian flags appeared in some groups. The flags got passed around the groups. We didn't really know whom they belonged to. But we waved them turn by turn anyway. By now John had started writing something, often looking at his iPad, as if he was referring to something. It was pretty strange thing to do but we didn't really pay any attention.

Just when it started looking like a nightmare for India, with Afridi and Misbah batting well, Afridi got out.

41.5 : Harbhajan Singh to Shahid Afridi, OUT, gone! Harbhajan sends down a high full toss, Afridi attempts to smash it baseball-style down the ground but the ball takes the top edge and swirls up for cover to take an easy catch. The captain departs, he had to go for his shots but couldn't execute that one too well. This is India's game now

Shahid Afridi c Sehwag b Harbhajan Singh 19 (25m 17b 1x4 0x6) SR: 111.76

Pakistan 184/7 Misbah-ul-Haq 26* (50b 1x4)

Harbhajan Singh 8.5-0-36-2

There was a loud roar again. After the dangerous Afridi was back in the pavilion, Indian fans knew victory was around the corner. Some fans actually started dancing to the rhythm of claps, whistles and banging tables. Someone ordered a super large pitcher and started pouring beer for everyone in the pub. It was chaos, cacophony and confusion but it was also camaraderie, togetherness and a strange sense of belonging. I had lost track of where John was and what he was upto.

The Pakistan players look utterly downcast in the dressing room. The dream was over

> *49.5 :Khan to Misbah-ul-Haq, OUT, there's the game! Misbah swings, the ball goes miles up in the air and lands safely in Kohli's hands at long-on*
>
> *Misbah-ul-Haq c Kohli b Khan 56 (134m 76b 5x4 1x6) SR: 73.68*

India win by 29 runs to reach a dream home final in Mumbai, where they will face Sri Lanka to decide the World Cup! Shahid Afridi leads his team out to shake hands with the victorious Indians. Pakistan players can certainly hold their heads up high after their performances in this tournament.

Finally, India won the match. The bar owner announced one last drink on the house. There was more shouting than drinking, more toasts than sips, more spirit of togetherness than spirit in the glasses. We had made new friends whose names we didn't know, we were likely to forget what they looked like and perhaps our paths may never cross but at that moment we were together, happy, celebrating, experiencing the same feeling.

Those, who knew how to live the moment, were on cloud nine. Those who didn't, were learning it fast. The binding force was cricket. Religion does the same thing, right? It binds unknown people by a common thread, creates a spirit of togetherness, and becomes the glue that brings people together. On that very evening, in Kuala Lumpur cricket had played the same role for hundred-odd Indians who had gathered in that old Irish pub. The feeling was priceless. We bid farewell to each other and started to walk off.

I went back to my table to collect my bag. There was no sign of John. I felt a little bad that I didn't say goodbye to him.

I was about to leave when I saw a handwritten note lying on the table where John was sitting. I was wonderstruck while reading the contents.

Why Do Indians love cricket?

In Cricket, each team member regardless of his skill level is assured a place in the limelight. It is not just the limelight but it's an opportunity to perform, which on a good day can be a life changing experience. Because, on his day, one exceptionally brilliant or motivated individual can defeat the entire team. Cricket does not favor any particular physical trait. Internationally successful cricketers come in all shapes and sizes. Even a handicapped player can be a world champion. No other game can offer this opportunity. Thus, Cricket offers the best chance for an underdog to hunt the powerful. What's more, you don't even need to play cricket to talk about it. Talking about cricket is probably more fun than actually playing it.

A common man in India is still an underdog. Daily life is nothing less than a struggle. Special world-class traits are rare, financial wherewithal is absent. Opportunities to perform are denied on the basis of caste, creed, class, religion, language, and physical traits. Being in the limelight is considered a once in a lifetime opportunity. No wonder the common man has developed a deep psychological connection with a game that assures opportunity to perform, offers equal chance of success without any bias and assures moments of limelight no matter what. They are fanatic because Cricket gives them things that their life can't... And they all love Sachin Tendulkar because for them he is dream in motion. They want to emulate him in a real life situation. They want to win singlehandedly against all odds. They want to be him.

Indians have a deep psychological connection with cricket. It is considered a religion in India and it would always stay that way.

I was speechless as I read it. It was so profound, so deep and so right. John must have been a gifted psychic man. He must have perhaps travelled around in India and therefore knew about struggles of Indians in their daily lives. Perhaps, he learnt about cricket in the last few hours and connected it so well. His analysis was spot-on. He had converted quick observations into profound connections and presented them in a crisp note.

Since that day, I started liking cricket even more. I understood the deeper mental connection that existed between this game and me. It became clear to me why I find it easy to explain a strategy to my team in cricket lingo. I understood the true meaning of a spontaneous sentence I said earlier in the day about where a legacy should belong. I was very clear why cricket was no longer a British legacy in India but rather India's calling card to the sports world. I am no longer apologetic about why India is a cricket-crazy nation.

But ever since that day, I kept searching for John in Kuala Lumpur. I went to the same pub again, I enquired about him but nobody knew who he was. They told he always came dressed in the same green half shirt and cargo trousers but they didn't know his name and where he lived.

If I meet him I want to ask him which country he was from and whether he had visited India before. I want to know how he learnt about the new game so quickly. I want to know how he derived such profound conclusions. I want to ask whether he left the note for me. I want to ask him if his name really was John. If you happen to see him please tell him to call me. He is a man of average height, tanned white skin, slim, on wrong side of 50, dressed in a loose green half shirt and cargo trousers, with a well- grown white beard.

Please let me know, will you?

5

WHY ARE INDIANS GOOD AT JUGAAD?

Have you watched the movie 'The Truman Show'? The protagonist Truman, played by Jim Carrey, is born in a reality show. He grows upon the movie sets under the illusion created by the director that the set is the real world. Each person around him is an actor and everything follows a pattern. The director thinks he has gifted a perfect world to Truman, a world that is predictable & safe, where everything is under control.

A few years ago, when I migrated from Bangalore to Singapore, I started feeling as if I was also Truman and Singapore was an ongoing Truman show. Everything was so predictable and safe, in complete contrast to India. Everything back home was chaotic. 'Firefighting' skills, ability to make sense out of chaos and being able to pave your own way were essential survival skills, just as important as breathing. Singapore on the other hand is always neat, clean and timely. Every time you turn on the tap, water flows. Every time you press the switch, the light comes on. And every time you unlock your smart phone, it connects to the Internet.

Initially, I struggled working in such an orderly atmosphere. Back home, planning was essential but not necessary, because whatever plans you made were only to measure the extent of deviation. The famous saying went : if everything is going exactly as planned, you are overlooking something very important.

I was used to getting things done at the last moment. We had coined a term for this. We used to call it 'SHIT' a.k.a. Some- How-In-Time. In Singapore, everyone around expected me to have a detailed plan and chances that everything would go as per the plan were very high. Trains, buses and taxis would arrive exactly as per schedule. The vendors delivered on the promised dates. Colleagues stuck to their deadlines and most projects got completed on time. It may sound silly but it was a big change of culture for me and I tried my best to adjust.

But all days are not the same. In 2008, the Lehman crash sent the global markets into a tailspin. There was unprecedented turbulence in the market. Our clients' sales plummeted, they cut down on their manpower and consulting budgets and soon we were in very choppy waters.

Although Singapore still functioned with its trademark predictability, our business became extremely unpredictable. The meetings from which we had walked out with big orders earlier, yielded nothing now. Clients who used to call us on their own, started avoiding us. Our meticulously designed plans were not working. In short - it was chaos.

Surprisingly, I started feeling very normal. I started enjoying being on my feet and making last minute clever decisions to push my way through again.

In India, we call this "*Jugaad*." *Jugaad*, a Hindi word, roughly means finding an innovative solution to a problem against harsh constraints. This solution is usually an out-of-the- box invention under resource constraints, specific to the situation or problem involved. A spark of brilliance originating out of unstructured ideas! Indians at home or abroad not just manage with, but relish this concept. Many of them, yours truly included attribute the ability to do *jugaad* as an important quality that helps them to succeed in their education, career, a particular job, or life in general. So far in Singapore, I was not required to use my 'jugaad-ability'. But the turbulence in the global market situation gave me the opportunity to use my well-honed skills once again.

I didn't have to wait long. With the chips down, every lead was important. We managed to get a lead, which was meant to be for an advertising agency rather than a consulting company like ours. On a normal day, we would not have touched it with a barge pole, but the deal value was high enough to help us meet our targets. My antennae were up and I was thinking out of the box to make it work.

"Boss, do you really think we can put in a credible bid for this?" asked Emily.

She was a bright colleague who had recently joined us and was learning very fast. She was one of the top sellers before the market had crashed but had lost all her wits in the turbulent period.

"Umm... I am not sure but we have to give it a shot." I knew we had to attempt this though I didn't know what we should do.

"We have never done this before. We don't have the required experience. How can we do it?" asked Simon. He usually asked just the right questions. He had just joined back after his honeymoon.

"Simon, you just got married, right?" I asked. "Yes Boss."

"Were you married before this? Did you have the required experience before marriage?" I asked, with a wink.

Sometimes humor can put even the most compelling argument to rest. All of us, except Simon, had a hearty laugh.

"This is only possible if we interpret the clients' requirements in a way that is suitable for us. We have to bring things to our turf rather than the competitor's" said Jee.

Jee was our Thai colleague who used to sympathize with my *jugaad* tendencies. According to her, developing markets could never function without it.

"That sounds great, but how can we do it?" asked Emily.

She would be the prime beneficiary if this worked out it.

"Well we need to harp on our market knowledge and contacts. Client's focus is on media. We have to make that part redundant. We have to convince the client that meeting the right people is more important than media presence," I was trying to build an argument as I went along.

Jee rejoined, "Yes. Their media budget is quite high, if we take this approach we can have enough of a budget for organizing roadshows, and we can even pass some savings back to the client."

"If we are cost effective, we can win this. I know the client is very price sensitive," the sales person in Emily was speaking.

"Well, then I will work on the approach that positions us as market experts and show the client that we could achieve better results at a lower cost," Simon said. The good thing about Simon was, once he overcame his skepticism, he was able to contribute wholeheartedly.

We had some follow up discussions to fine-tune our offerings and the team was ready. Needless to say, this *jugaad* done under adverse market conditions paid rich dividends. We won that prestigious contract against an ad agency. Under normal conditions we would have overlooked this opportunity, but scarcity and an adverse situation forced us to think creatively and to come up with a *jugaad* solution to win this contract.

After the sweet win, we had a small party thrown by our Singapore office manager, who was all praises for the team. After a couple of drinks, he took me aside for a private chat.

"How did you even get this idea to position us this way? My straight-jacketed thinking is still not able to come to terms with this win. I still can't understand how you convinced the client," He was full of praise.

"Thanks Boss, we are flattered." I was trying to be humble.

"No. No. No. Don't be humble. You Indians are absolutely brilliant at this. Whenever there are uncertainties or grey areas, you guys come up with some brilliant solution," Either he was drunk or was in a very generous mood or both.

"We struggle to come up with any such ideas. How are you able to think so independently? How are you able to work in chaos so easily?" He had many questions. I didn't have a convincing answer. I somehow escaped from this but it certainly got me thinking.

It is true that Indians are good at *jugaad*. It is true that we thrive in grey areas, ambiguous situations and often come up with solutions that are new. Is it because we grow up under all kinds of constraints and that *jugaad* is the only way to gather the resources we need? Or are we taught and encouraged to think differently? I read stories on the Internet about how Punjabi *dhabawalas* (highway restaurant owners) used washing machines to make Lassi - a *jugaad* innovation among many other examples. I also notice a few books written on *jugaad* as a type of innovation. Although everyone is in awe, not everyone appreciates *jugaad*. There is a group in our office that looks down upon every *jugaad* innovation. For them it is simply bending the rules by interpreting them differently. For them, these are temporary measures that can't be reused in other situations, or in short, institutionalized.

I realize that *jugaad* exists in some form or the other in other developing countries too. But one thing that clearly stands out - there is no other country in the world except India where *jugaad* is the first option for a solution. There is no other country where *jugaad* solution designers command respect or are looked up to. The ability to come up with a *jugaad* solution may exist everywhere but it is the glamor and authenticity of such solutions in India that stands out. This in fact draws more and more people to contribute actively to *jugaad* solutions and it becomes a perpetual cycle.

What makes Indians good at *jugaad*? Or why does it have such legitimacy in India? Why do people look up to it? Why is *jugaad* so glorified in India?

The popular answers include lack of resources and an inefficient system, to name just a few. Some say it is the propensity to break the law. Some attribute it to the intelligence of Indians. While all these are necessary reasons, none of them make India or Indians unique. None of them address the questions raised above comprehensively. None of them explains why people look up to *jugaad*. I was not hoping to find an answer to this profound question without any research, advice or serious soul searching. But I stumbled upon a possible profound answer accidentally.

One night, I was reading a story to my son about Lord Ganesha and his brother Lord Kartikeya.

Their parents, Lord Shankar and Goddess Parvati, once asked their sons - Ganesha & Kartikeya to race around the world. The one who came back first would be declared the winner. Ganesha was fat and rode a mouse. Kartikeya was fit and rode a peacock. Kartikeya was sure to win. As soon as the race started Kartikeya flew off on his peacock. Ganesha and his mouse moved very slowly. Ganesha knew he would lose the race for sure. But then he thought of an out of the box idea. He went around his parents three times (This is called a *'pradakshina'* in Sanskrit. It is usually done in temples to the God. This is how you pay your respects to the god.) Ganesha then wittily declared that doing three *pradakshinas* around his godly parents was as good as going around the world. This flattering explanation pleased his parent and they declared him the winner. Kartikeya went around the world literally, which obviously took much longer, and was declared to have lost the race.

I concluded the story. But my son looked unconvinced. "How unfair is that!" exclaimed my five year old, "Forget winning, he didn't even run the race."

I had heard this story since my childhood and never thought of questioning it. I had always admired Ganesha's intelligence, by which he could think of such a brilliant idea. But the fact remains that he didn't actually run the race. My son was right. We hate to call it *jugaad* out of respect for the gods, but if the same story was told with characters named A, B and C, it would clearly be a story of *jugaad*.

My son went off to sleep but I was wide awake. All the stories I had heard in my childhood and accepted without questioning, started playing in my mind. All these stories had helped me define what is right and what is wrong. They were a part of me now.

Another such story is that of 'Hiranyakashyapu'. Hiranyakashyapu was a powerful demon king. He was enemy of Lord Vishnu, as Lord Vishnu had killed his brother in Varah avatar (incarnation in the form of a boar). Hiranyakashyapu did a penance - several years of austerity and continuous prayers - to Lord Brahma. Lord Brahma was pleased, and granted him a boon. Hiranyakashyapu asked for immortality, which Brahma refused. So instead he asked for a death, which was subject to various difficult conditions. As Bhagavat Puran (one of the oldest and greatest Sanskrit Puranic texts of Hinduism) describes,

"O my lord, O best of the givers of benediction, if you will kindly grant me the benediction I desire, please let me not meet death from any of the living entities created by you.

Grant me that I not die within any residence or outside any residence, during the daytime or at night, nor on the ground or in the sky. Grant me that my death not be brought by any being other than those created by you, nor by any weapon, nor by any human being or animal.

Grant me that I not meet death from any entity, living or nonliving. Grant me, further, that I not be killed by any demigod or demon or by any great snake from the lower planets. Since no one can kill you in the battlefield, you have no competitor. Therefore, grant me the benediction that I too may have no rival. Give me sole lordship over all the living entities and presiding deities, and give me all the glories obtained by that position. Furthermore, give me all the mystic powers attained by long austerities and the practice of yoga, for these cannot be lost at any time."

With such a big boon he became very powerful and arrogant. The Gods could not defeat him and were losing ground each day. Killing him became an impossible task. So Vishnu donned the avatar (incarnation) of Narasimha - half human, half lion - appeared from a broken column in the evening – neither day nor night - and killed Hiranyakashyapu with his long nails - which can't be termed as weapons. Thus his death defied all the stringent conditions by an innovative borderline solution - *Jugaad*.

During the famous war of Mahabharata, Bhishma was undefeatable. But he had taken a vow that he would fight only men. So the Pandavas brought in a transgendered warrior, Shikhandi, to fight Bhishma. Bhishma could not fight Shikhandi due to his vow, and put down his arms. Arjuna fired arrows hiding behind Shikhandi and defeated Bhishma. This was nothing else but quintessential *jugaad*. Drona was the Pandavas' teacher. It was difficult for the Pandavas to defeat him. So they killed an elephant, who had the same name as Drona's son - Ashwatthama and spread the news that Ashwatthama was killed. Hearing this, Drona thought his son was no more and dropped his weapons in sorrow. He was then beheaded, breaching the rules of the war of not killing an unarmed man. Each of these strategies contained a single crucial ingredient - *jugaad*.

All these stories form the foundations of childhood of many Indians. Even non-Hindu Indians would have heard these stories as they grew up. We tell these stories to our children to help them decipher what is right and what is wrong. In each of these stories, *jugaad* is glorified, legitimized and worshipped. No wonder, this way of independent thinking, personal interpretation of rules and regulations, is considered the key to success. No wonder *jugaad* is considered legitimate. No wonder we look up to it and no wonder that we are good at it.

Although we are good at *jugaad*, it is not our key to success for a better tomorrow. *Jugaad* does give Indians an edge especially in uncertain situations. Most clients and colleagues notice that Indians tend to be independent thinkers and are likely to bring in an out-of-the-box perspective. But just like any tool, *jugaad* can be immensely beneficial only if used in the right way. Indians should be aware that *jugaad* is not an established concept in the global context. In most cases, it is looked down upon. It is seen as an excuse to bend rules and a justification to take short cuts. Most of the first world countries are governed by strict rules and bending the rules is considered as violating them unlike in India, where rules might have a lot of executional ambiguity.

Having spent a considerable time within and outside India, having worked in several cultures, and with some world class companies, I have learnt that although *jugaad* brought us till here, it may not take us very far. In this era of the pursuit of perfection, *Jugaad* may no doubt give you a head start but a quick transition to a systematic planned way of working within the rules is very essential. This is not an era of quick fix solutions. A *jugaad* mindset is good for quick fixes but unfortunately it comes in the way of the pursuit of excellence. The *jugaad* mindset takes you in the opposite direction. So my message to my fellow Indians and Indian enterprises is that, as soon as you have crossed initial hurdles you should abandon the *jugaad* mindset and pursue excellence. You should avoid the temptation of following the same mindset.

In most cases what got you there, may not take you further. *Jugaad* is surely one of them.

ABOUT THE AUTHOR

Vivek Vaidya is a management consultant by profession, appears on major TV Channels like BBC, CNBC, Bloomberg, Al Jazeera, ET Now, Channel News Asia as Automotive Expert, delivers keynote speeches on diverse topics across the world but is a blogger at heart. He blogs on everyday happenings to bring out hidden perspectives that are invisible in foresight but obvious in hindsight. Buoyed by his response to a blog about inscrutable Indian habits and practices, he decided to write a book about it. The book blends entertaining anecdotal perspectives coupled with insights arising out of being a global Indian. This book has already received excellent response in pre-publishing phase by way of forewords from opinion makers and rave reviews from friends

"Why Do Indians...?" is the book that is likely to make you laugh, entertain, be sensitive and introspect at the same time.

Enjoy his maiden venture in the world of books!!

WHERE TO FIND VIVEK VAIDYA ONLINE

- Website: www.vivekvaidya.com
- Twitter: www.twitter.com/mrvivekvaidya
- Facebook: www.facebook.com/mr.vivekvaidya
- LinkedIn: www.linkedin.com/in/vaidyavivek
- Blog: www.vivekvaidya.com